# Target Practice

## A Teacher's Resource for ASL Games and Activities

M. Lynn Woolsey

Butte Publications, Inc.
Hillsboro, Oregon, USA

# Target Practice
A Teacher's Resource for Games and Activities

Copyright © 1998 M. Lynn Woolsey

Design: Anita Jones

All rights reserved.  Only the pages of this book specifically marked may be reproduced or transmitted in any form or by any means without permission in writing from the publisher.

**Reproducible pages include:**

| | | |
|---|---|---|
| Signal Flags | Page 13 | Blank grid for Flags |
| It's a Gift for You | Page 17 | Gift Ideas |
| Charades with Feeling | Page 20 | Feelings List |
| Story Group Scenes | Pages 25-30 | Scenes |
| And Who Are You? | Pages 32-34 | Identity Cards |
| Dayrunning | Pages 48-53 | Calendars |
| Ailment and Cure Cards | Pages 69-74 | Ailments and Cures |
| The McGreevy Family | Pages 84,85 | Family Tree & Blank |
| | Pages 90,91 | Family Relationship Cards |
| Ask the Experts | Pages 93-98 | Biographies |
| | Pages 100-102 | Business Cards |
| | Page 104 | Student Directions |
| None of Your Business | Pages 111-115 | Business Cards |
| | Pages 121-126 | Errands |

Butte Publications, Inc.
P.O. Box 1328
Hillsboro, OR 97123-1328
U.S.A.

ISBN 1-884362-29-X

## *Dedication*

To my children, Elizabeth, Meredith and Christopher.
They are magic.


To my parents who told me I could do anything.
They believed and so did I.

# ACKNOWLEDGMENTS

During the transitions from ideas to drafts to manuscripts I have been blessed with whatever was needed to make *Target Practice* a reality.

My deepest thanks go to Christy Stone who served as the original catalyst for this book. Dr. David Halstead and the Vancouver School District provided me with early support for the book and reasons to persevere. Kristin Kautz and Pat Flynn were invaluable resources in the early stages when I needed books and feedback. Without the computer genius of James McGreevy and Dee Rains this book would still be stuck on some unreadable and incompatible floppy disk! Roseann Jones, Andrina Kalita, Katrina Mathews and Julia Taylor were always ready in the early days to brainstorm lists or copy something for me. Chanel Carlascio invested hours of her own time trying to decipher and then edit my initial draft. Endless thanks go to my sign language students who laughingly endured many "unusual" games which, fortunately, did not survive the final editing. My good friends Bill Alsdurf and Jer Loudenback proved to be constant sources of support to me. Maddie Hartwell, "angel at large," filled in some of the necessary blanks and reminded me about the difference between my work and myself. My attorneys Turid Owren and Diana Hodge helped me navigate the legal path to publication. Margaret Walworth, my original editor, shared her editorial talent as well as her calm and peaceful spirit with me. Dr. William Brelje, his caretaking approach to people and his peaceful cabin in the woods provided the perfect environment for completion of the final manuscript. My mother selflessly offered her time and energy. She copied and collated pages, shared my burdens and quietly allowed me to rely on her strength. Matthew Brink shared my vision, my frustrations, and his resources to make Target Practice a reality. Finally, I wish to thank Gary Rollins and Ann Flannery who are rare friends, indeed. Glimpses of their spirits and spirituality are evident in the pages you are about to read.

# TABLE OF CONTENTS

**Preface** ...vii

**Introduction** ...viii

**Bows and Arrows   15 Minute Games** ...7
- Which Way? ...9
- Signal Flags ...11
- Signs of the Times ...14
- It's a Gift for You ...16
- The House that Jack Built ...18
- Charades with Feeling ...19

**Bull's Eye   15-30 Minute Games** ...21
- Story Groups ...23
- And Who are You? ...31
- Develop a Survey ...35
- Now You See It, Now You Don't ...37
- What's Inside? ...39
- Categories ...40
- Who Owns the Gallery? ...42
- Jen and Maggie's Schedule ...44
- Outpatient Clinics ...45
- Dayrunning ...47
- Kiddie Kare Fingerpainting "Faux Pas" ...54
- Twenty Year Reunion ...55
- Chore Chart ...57
- Gretchen's "To Do" List ...58
- Employment Agency Networking ...60
- Oils and Aromas ...62
- Healing Stones ...64
- Mother's Nature Remedies ...66
- Cure It Naturally ...68
- Hypochondriac ...69
- Miracle Cures! ...69
- How Much, How Many Survey ...76
- Out To Lunch ...78
- Personal Time Lines ...79
- The Weekend ...80
- Wacko Weddings ...81

**Target Range   30-50 Minute Games** ...83
- The Mcgreevy Family Tree ...85
- Ask The Experts ...95
- None Of Your Business ...113

**Index** ...141

v

 # PREFACE

When I was teaching American Sign Language (ASL) in a public high school to hearing students I discovered quickly that in order to keep their interest and facilitate their learning process, I had to provide the students with something more than "drill and kill" exercises after a lesson. My students had no intention of doing anything "boring" or rigidly structured. They wanted *fun, excitement, thrills.*

Those three words do not exactly describe the typical foreign language classroom. Often, learning a foreign language is repetitive, functionally based and somewhat dry.

I was uninterested in teaching ASL in the same way other foreign languages were taught. I searched all the available material I could find related to sign language games and activities. Several books I found were ancient and out of print. The newer activities were enjoyable but I wanted more variety. It was then that I turned to books with a focus on English as a Second Language. Those materials provided a wealth of information upon which I could improvise. During the following years, I developed the games and activities you will find in this book.

Play was a powerful motivator for my ASL students. I witnessed a remarkable shift in students' perception of learning. Through the games we set ourselves free to play with each other and with the language. With a focus on play, attitudes shifted. We created a safe environment for ourselves. We learned how to share our struggles, victories and setbacks. We risked and we grew.

During those years I was fortunate. I saw magic in my classroom. I believe that *Target Practice* is one of the magic ingredients that contributes to a successful ASL classroom. The games and activities are designed to provide enjoyable and even sublimely ridiculous opportunities for practicing some of the necessary skills needed to support the development of fluency in ASL. So, cut loose, play and step back to witness magic!

# INTRODUCTION

## TO THE TEACHER

*Target Practice* is designed to offer students an opportunity to develop and practice expressive and receptive skills in American Sign Language. The games and activities are intended to be used to supplement a sign language text. The games and activities in *Target Practice* are designed to be played exclusively in ASL. There is no place for spoken English in any of the games.

Each of the games and activities has been tested in classrooms with high school students as well as adults. You may find that some of the games fit your style of teaching perfectly. You may find that other games are not exactly suited to your particular teaching style or to your personality. I encourage you to adapt the games to suit the needs of you and your students! If students are smiling and signing, magic is happening!

You may be surprised to see that some of the games and activities border on the ridiculous! Interestingly, I found that it is easier for some students to take a risk when EVERYONE is expected to act and look silly. You may also notice that some of the games clearly reflect a "hearing" and rather corny sense of humor. Since *Target Practice* is designed for hearing students, these games serve well as a catalyst for conversations about language, culture, values and humor.

The information related to several activities, including but not limited to *Mother's Nature's Remedies, Cure it Naturally, Hypochondriac, Miracle Cures* and *Oils and Aromas* is only intended to serve to enhance the practice of ASL within a reality-based context. The information is in no way intended to serve in any capacity in the place of professional health care. The author and publisher assume no legal responsibility for the advice and information contained within.

 # THE LAYOUT

*Target Practice* is divided into three sections by time.

**Bows and Arrows    15 Minute Games**

The games in this section can be completed in approximately 15 minutes, although the time can be easily extended. Typically these games do not require much target language use, nor do they require extended visual attention. I have used these games as ice-breaker activities, as warm-up or transition exercises, as readiness activities, for specific review, to identify improvement over time, as comic relief, and as lessons for advanced students to teach.

**Bull's Eye    15-30 Minute Games**

Games in this section are designed to serve as instructional support for specific lessons. However, they are flexible enough so that they can be easily adapted to fit many different skills and concepts. The length of time required for these games allows students the chance to engage with each other and in the game using ASL without worrying about time constraints. The duration of these activities also allows the teacher time to evaluate student skills.

**Target Range    20-50 Minute Games**

Games in this section are divided into units. Each unit contains several activities of varying difficulty. These units are designed to be played over the course of a student's ASL development. Begin with the easy activities in the early part of the year. As the skills of the students improve, return to more challenging games in the unit. I found that each time we returned to the unit, the students' increased familiarity with the unit and its characters generated an increase in comfort. That comfort generated more risk-taking and more learning.

Many of the activities in this section focus on role play which has a great deal of flexibility as well as a rather unique and unpredictable nature. The addition of props and costumes increases student participation as well as their enjoyment!

# THE ACTIVITIES

Since many of the activities in *Target Practice* are task-oriented, students focus their attention on the use and application of the language in situations that can mirror real life. This allows for a natural approach to the communication process.

Each game or activity contains a description of the following criteria at the top of the page in this Teacher's Resource.

**Practice Targets**
**Level**
**Group Size**
**Repeat**
**Materials**
**Preparation**
**Background**
**Directions**

**Practice Targets:** A description of the possible areas of practice. The first entry is most prominent in the game. The following entries are involved in the activity but to a lesser extent. A complete list of the skill areas covered in the *Target Practice* activities can be found on page 4.

**Level:** The level of skill required for the game is denoted by stars.

★         Virtually no sign language required

★★       Some sign language recommended

★★       Intermediate sign language skills recommended

★★★★ A working fluency with the language recommended

**Group Sizes:** Group sizes are defined as follows:

   *Large Groups:* typically the whole class or more than five students

   *Small Groups:* are limited to 3 - 5 students

   *Pairs:* involve two students

**Repeat:** Some of the games can be played only once. These games are indicated by a **no**. Other games can be played many times and are indicated by a **yes**.

**Materials:** The materials required for the game are listed in each entry.

**Preparation:** Any work that must be completed prior to the students' arrival in class is listed under this heading.

**Background:** Sometimes background information is included to add realism to the activity. This information is included in the student workbook as well.

**Directions:** Directions for each activity are included in this section. For ease of identification and clarification the pronoun "she" is used for teachers and "he" for students.

# PRACTICE TARGETS

## Readiness

- visual/gestural comfort
- mirror image vs. visual reverse
- pantomime
- visual attending
- visual memory
- eye contact

## Descriptors

- classifiers
- spatial relationships
- inflection

## Structures

- simple sentence
- Y/N question
- Wh- question
- Rh- question
- plurals
- existential "have"
- pronouns
  regular
  indexing/determiners
  possessive
- negation
- command
- conditional
- topicalization
- comparative
- verb agreement
- subject/object agreement
- conjunctions

## Time

- past
- present
- future
- habitual

## Numerals

- time (clock, calendar, schedules, etc.)
- quantities (counting, math, measurement, etc.)
- order
- money

## Discourse

- requesting attention
- beginning/ending conversations
- affirming/confirming
- clarifying strategies
- turn-taking
- register variation

## Articulation

- movement
- handshape
- location
- palm orientation
- non-manual signals
- place & manner
- noun/verb distinction
- fingerspelling

 # THE STUDENT WORKBOOK

The Student Workbook provides pages and pages of focused ASL practice activities. Directions for the games are included in the workbook. Using this format you can either explain the directions in ASL to the students and immediately begin the activities, request that the students read the directions themselves or use a combination of both. Activities that do not require a workbook page are included in the Teacher's Manual only.

Many of the activities require students to write some information on the workbook page. Encourage students to either draw a picture of the information or to use brief notes instead of English sentences.

Several of the activities are designed to be played by two people. The workbook page of one partner typically contains the information that the other partner needs. At times, workbook pages should be kept private.

In some cases, the workbook pages can be used several times. In many cases the completed workbook pages of partners or groups will be identical. In cases such as this, students can hand in their worksheets for assessment. In a few situations, students will be asked to use their own paper for an activity.

 # SAFE ENVIRONMENT

Anxiety can be a significant barrier to successful language learning. The teacher who designs a safe environment in the classroom will find that students, particularly adults, will be more likely to take risks.

- Be sure that all students understand the directions. Find ways to ensure their success in each of the activities.

- Encourage students to improvise if they do not know a sign. While it is inappropriate for students to invent a sign, encourage them to develop some skills in using body language and pantomime.

- Take advantage of opportunities to model the correct use of the language.

- Ask for volunteers instead of calling on students.

- Help students change their perception about "failures." Failures are really stepping stones to fluency in ASL.

- Remember that frustrated students are less able to process information. Sometimes it makes sense to offer students the answer rather than increase their level of frustration.

- Offer strategies for independent learning. Encourage students to use each other, textbooks, dictionaries; whatever works.

- Whenever possible, explain to students why you are playing each of the games and what they can lean from the game.

- Add props whenever possible! They add reality and fun to the lessons.

- In a safe environment, students can teach each other.

- Remember that enthusiasm and patience are contagious!

# BOWS AND ARROWS

## 15 Minute Activities

The games in this section can be completed in approximately 15 minutes, although the time can be easily extended. Typically these games do not require much target language use, nor do they require extended visual attention. These games can be used as ice-breaker activities, as warm-up or transition exercises, as readiness activities, for specific review, to identify improvement over time, as comic relief, and as lessons for advanced students to teach.

 # BOWS AND ARROWS

## WHICH WAY?

**Practice Targets:** Readiness, Discourse, Descriptors, Articulation
**Level:** ★
**Group Size:** Varies
**Repeat:** Yes
**Materials:** Student Workbook pages 2, 3, an extra sheet of paper for Activity 3, and a pencil
**Preparation:** None

### ACTIVITY 1   TEACHER DESCRIPTIONS

**Directions:** For this activity you will use the arrows on the Student Workbook page. One by one, describe each of the arrows to the students, drawing special attention to the direction of each arrow. Encourage students to follow along on the Workbook page while you introduce the differences between mirror images and directions of movement.

Next, select several arrows in a random order. Describe each arrow to the class. Instruct students to make a number one (1) in the right top corner in the box of the first arrow you describe. Describe the second arrow to the students. They will mark a number two (2) in the box which corresponds to that arrow. Continue in this manner until you have described each of the arrows.

### ACTIVITY 2   STUDENT ARROWS

**Directions:** Ask for a student volunteer to choose and describe one of the arrows from the Workbook page. Instruct the rest of the class to record a number one (1) in the top left corner of the box of the arrow that they believe corresponds to the student volunteer's description. If students are confused, teach them how to ask for clarification. The student volunteer will then offer the correct answer and ask for a second student volunteer. The second volunteer will describe another arrow, offer clarification if requested, give the answer and ask for a third student volunteer. Students in the class will continue to mark their numbers in the left corners of the corresponding arrow boxes. Continue until all of the arrows have been described.

 **BOWS AND ARROWS**

## *WHICH WAY?*

### ACTIVITY 3   SMALL GROUP DESCRIPTIONS

**Materials:** A sheet of paper and pencil for each student

**Directions:** Assign students to small groups. Instruct each member to take a turn describing an arrow to the group. Each group member will draw the arrow they see described. After each turn group members will compare their drawings to the correct arrow and make any necessary changes. Play continues until each of the arrows has been described.

### REPLICA OF *WHICH WAY?* FROM STUDENT WORKBOOK - PAGE 3

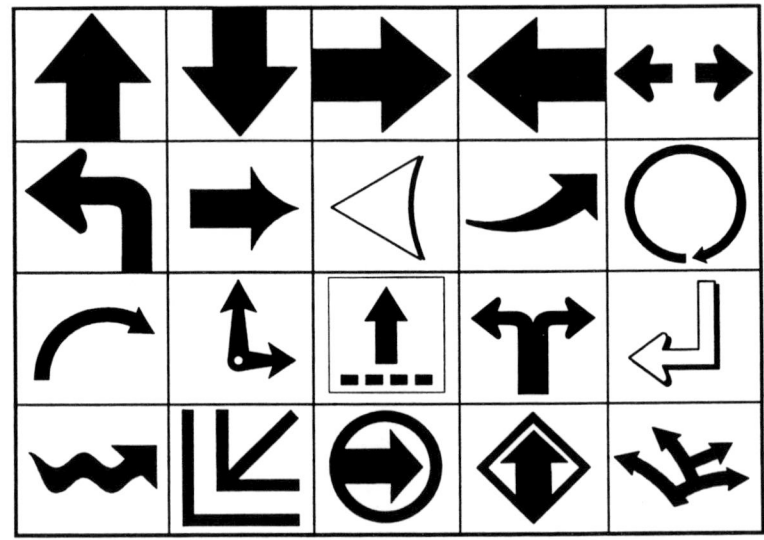

10

 # BOWS AND ARROWS

## SIGNAL FLAGS

**Practice Targets:** Readiness, Discourse, Descriptors, Articulation
**Level:** ★
**Group Size:** Varies
**Repeat:** Yes
**Materials:** Teacher's Manual Signal Flag Key, Student Workbook pages 4, 5, 6, pencil, crayons, extra paper for Activity 4
**Preparation:** None

### Background Information

The flags used for this activity are part of the International Flag Code which consists of over forty flags. Messages are sent to other ships by hoisting one of five flags which either spell out words or have coded meanings. For example, a ship in harbor would hoist the "P" flag if it is ready to set sail. The flags "I" and "T" together send the message that the ship is on fire. Ships carry books in nine languages that are used to decipher the codes.

### ACTIVITY 1   DRAW THE FLAGS

**Directions:** Note that the Student Workbook page is blank except for the examples. Choose a signal flag from the Teacher's Manual and describe it to the class. Instruct students to draw what they see. Compare the answer with the drawings of the students. Describe the remaining flags one by one, allowing students time for comparison and corrections.

### ACTIVITY 2   COLOR THE FLAGS

**Directions:** After students have drawn the flags, return to the page and invent the colors of each of the flags. Students will color each of the flags. If crayons are unavailable, students can simply write a letter that corresponds to a color in the appropriate area of the flag. For example, "B" means black, "R" means red, etc. students will describe their flags in a small group and compare answers.

### ACTIVITY 3   STUDENT DESCRIPTIONS

**Directions:** Using the key in the Teacher's Manual, ask for a student volunteer to describe one of the flags. Classmates can either point to the appropriate flag already drawn or mark numbers in the flag boxes. Continue with volunteers until each of the flags has been described.

# BOWS AND ARROWS

## SIGNAL FLAGS

### ACTIVITY 4   GROUP FLAGS

**Materials:** Several sheets of paper per student, pencil

**Directions:** Assign students to small groups. Instruct each group to meet together and create their own group flag. When the group flags are completed, each student will copy their group flag onto one of the sheets of paper.

After each group has created a flag, instruct students to pair up with a student from a different group. Each student in the pair will describe their group's flag to their partner who will draw the flag. Partners will reverse roles. When both partners have a copy of the other's flag, they will seed out a student from a different group and repeat the process. The activity continues until each student has a copy of every group flag.

**Note: For additional practice in this area, consider using flags from different countries.**

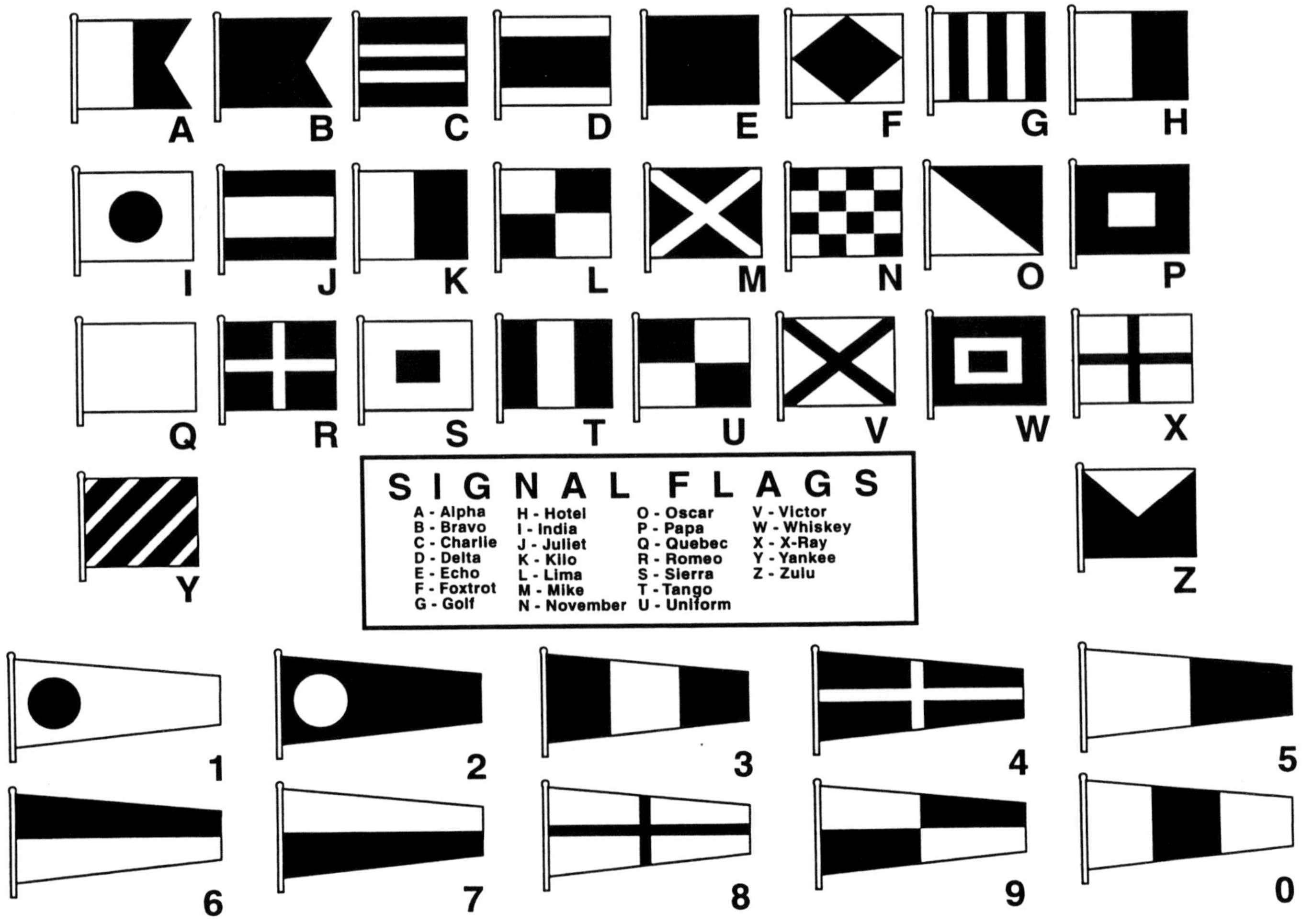

SIGNAL FLAGS

| A - Alpha | H - Hotel | O - Oscar | V - Victor |
|---|---|---|---|
| B - Bravo | I - India | P - Papa | W - Whiskey |
| C - Charlie | J - Juliet | Q - Quebec | X - X-Ray |
| D - Delta | K - Kilo | R - Romeo | Y - Yankee |
| E - Echo | L - Lima | S - Sierra | Z - Zulu |
| F - Foxtrot | M - Mike | T - Tango | |
| G - Golf | N - November | U - Uniform | |

THIS PAGE REPRODUCIBLE FOR CLASSROOM USE ONLY.

 **BOWS AND ARROWS**

## SIGNAL FLAGS

EXAMPLES FROM STUDENT WORKBOOK - PAGE 6

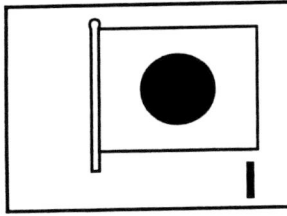
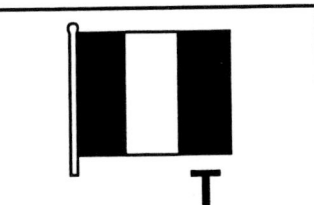

THIS PAGE REPRODUCIBLE FOR CLASSROOM USE ONLY.

13

# BOWS AND ARROWS

## SIGNS OF THE TIMES

**Practice Targets:** Readiness, Discourse, Descriptors
**Level:** ★
**Group Size:** Large
**Repeat:** Yes
**Materials:** Student Workbook pages 7, 8, pencil, extra paper for Activity 3
**Preparation:** None

### ACTIVITY 1    TEACHER DESCRIPTIONS

**Directions:** One by one describe each of the road signs to the students, drawing special attention to the shape of each sign and their unique qualities. Encourage the students to follow along on the Workbook page.

After each of the signs has been described, select several signs and present them in a random order. Describe your first choice to the class. Instruct students to mark a number one (1) in the top right corner of the box which corresponds to that road sign. Offer clarification and the answer when students are ready. Describe your second road sign choice to the class and ask them to mark a number two (2) in the top right corner of the road sign box. Continue in this manner until you have described each of the road signs.

- As a review choose a road sign and describe it. Ask students to identify the sign by the number they previously recorded in the top right or left corner.

### ACTIVITY 2    STUDENT DESCRIPTIONS

**Directions:** Ask for a student volunteer to choose and describe one of the signs from the Workbook page. Instruct the rest of the class to record a number one (1) in the top left corner of the box of the road sign they believe corresponds to the student volunteer's description. If a student in the class appears confused, show the class how to ask for and give clarification. After clarification has been given, the student volunteer can give the answer to the class and ask for a second volunteer. The second volunteer will describe a different road sign, offer clarification if requested, give the answer and ask for a third volunteer. Students in the class will continue to mark their numbers in the left corner of the road sign boxes. Play will continue until all of the road signs have been described.

- As a review ask a student volunteer to choose a road sign and describe it. Ask students to identify the sign by the number they previously recorded in the top right or left corner.

# BOWS AND ARROWS

## ACTIVITY 3   SMALL GROUP DESCRIPTIONS

**Materials:** Sheet of paper and pencil
**Directions:** Assign students to small groups. Instruct each member to take a turn describing a road sign to the group. Each group member will privately draw the road sign they see described. After each turn, group members will compare their drawings and make any necessary changes. Play continues until each of the road signs have been described.

### EXTENSION

**Materials:** The Student Workbook page used in Activity 1 and Activity 2
Pair students. Choose either the left or the right corner to use as a reference to the road sign. One student will sign a number that corresponds to a road sign. The other student will respond by describing the road sign. After each turn students will check for accuracy.

## REPLICA OF *SIGNS OF THE TIMES* FROM STUDENT WORKBOOK - PAGE 8

15

 # BOWS AND ARROWS

## IT'S A GIFT FOR YOU

**Practice Targets:** Readiness, Discourse, Descriptors
**Level:** ★
**Group Size:** Large or small
**Repeat:** Yes
**Materials:** Gift box, *Gift Ideas*
**Preparation:** Gift wrap a box so that the top can be easily opened or removed. Copy, cut and laminate the *Gift Ideas* and place them in the gift box.

**Directions:** Arrange the class so that everyone can see the gift box. Using pantomime skills, show the box to the class as though you have just received a special gift. Open the box and take out one of the gift ideas. Read the gift idea. Demonstrate the function of the gift and a distinctive feature. Show an emotional response to the gift.

Ask students to guess the object by creating their own pantomime of the gift, its function and feature. If there is some doubt about the student's guess, ask for clarification. Once a student has correctly guessed the gift pass the box to a student who will choose a gift idea, pantomime a function, a feature and a response.

Continue in this manner until time is up.

### VARIATION

Consider using the box near holidays such as Halloween, Valentine's Day or a student's birthday. Consider using *The Worst Christmas Gift* as the topic. Students can generate their own ideas when they open the gift box.

 # BOWS AND ARROWS

## IT'S A GIFT FOR YOU
### GIFT IDEAS

| 35 mm CAMERA | NEW PUPPY | UMBRELLA | CALCULATOR |
|---|---|---|---|
| BRIEFCASE | CD | PICTURE FRAME | FLOWERS |
| POCKET KNIFE | EXERCISE WORKOUT TAPE | VASE | BASEBALL CAP |
| IN-LINE SKATES | APRON | SILKY P.J.'S | EARRINGS & RING |
| CANDLE | PAINTS & BRUSHES | BLANKET | BABY SNAKE |
| GAME BOY | MONEY | POCKET WATCH | SOCKS & UNDERWEAR |
| POCKET PROTECTOR | SLIPPERS | STICKS OF INCENSE | BUBBLE BATH |

 # BOWS AND ARROWS

## THE HOUSE THAT JACK BUILT

**Practice Targets:** Readiness, Descriptors, Discourse
**Level:** ★★
**Group Size:** Large group first, then small groups or pairs
**Repeat:** Yes
**Materials:** None
**Preparation:** Clear a space in the room.

**Directions:** In this activity members of the class will use pantomime skills to create an imaginary room complete with furniture and appliances. Depending on the level of the students you may even choose to add smaller items such as lamps, vases and figurines.

Choose a room in a house. Begin the activity by using your pantomime skills to outline the walls, windows and the doorways. Demonstrate one of the major furniture pieces in the room such as a chair. Remember to describe its size and shape. Show its relationship to the walls, windows and the doors. Pantomime the use of the chair by sitting comfortably or stiffly in it.

Once you have described the room and the chair, ask a student volunteer to enter the *room* using the *door*. The student will repeat the pantomime description of the room by outlining the walls, windows and doorways. The student will copy your pantomime of the chair and sit in it as you did. The student will then pantomime another piece of furniture to add the room. The student will show its size, shape, its relationship to the walls, windows, doors and the chair. The student will use both pieces of furniture.

A third volunteer will repeat the pantomime of the room, the two pieces of furniture, and their relationship to the room and each other. He will then add one more object to the room.

Typically a little story develops along with the room. As the pantomime progresses it is increasingly easy to become confused. Ask the student volunteer to *freeze*. Ask the previous students to clarify the furniture location or the story line. Play continues until time is up.

 **BOWS AND ARROWS**

## CHARADES WITH FEELING

**Practice Targets:** Readiness, Discourse
**Level:** ★★
**Group Size:** Small group
**Repeat:** Yes
**Materials:** Feeling Cards, a hat
**Preparation:** Copy the *Feeling Cards*, cut out the feeling cards, and laminate them if you choose. Place them in the *hat*.

**Directions:** Place the *Feeling Cards* in the *hat*. Assign students to teams of four. Instruct one person from each group to leave the room. Pass the *hat* to each group. One member will choose one of the feelings from the *hat*. While their team member is waiting in the hall the group will read the feeling on the card and plan a pantomime skit that will demonstrate that emotion.

The team member who was waiting in the hall will return when his group is ready. When he returns, the three remaining group members will pantomime their skit. The student from the hall will guess the emotion by fingerspelling or signing.

Once the student has guessed the feeling, the process is repeated. The activity continues in this manner until time is up.

**Helpful Hints:**

- The first time the game is played, you may want to play it as a class.

- For beginning students, consider limiting the number of feelings that are in the *hat* and list them on the board.

- The game can become competitive by assigning each group the same emotion and using a stop watch to determine which group is fastest.

 # BOWS AND ARROWS

## CHARADES WITH FEELINGS
**FEELINGS LIST**

| | | | |
|---|---|---|---|
| AWED | TEMPTED | INTIMIDATED | CHILDLIKE |
| PRESSURED | JOYOUS | IMPATIENT | MELANCHOLY |
| JEALOUS | CONTENTED | PANICKED | GREEDY |
| RESENTFUL | RESTLESS | SILLY | HYPER |
| SHOCKED | IGNORED | LOVED | KIND |
| OBNOXIOUS | CONFUSED | PROUD | EXHAUSTED |
| DISTRACTED | GUILTY | PRISSY | DEPRESSED |
| PASSIONATE | INTELLIGENT | ANGRY | FEARFUL |

# BULL'S EYE

## 15 - 30 Minute Activities

Games in this section are designed to serve as instructional support for specific lessons. However, they are flexible enough so that they can be easily adapted to fit many different skills and concepts. The length of time required for these games allows students the chance to engage with each other and in the game using ASL without worrying about time constraints. The duration of these activities also allows the teacher time to evaluate student skills.

# BULL'S EYE

## STORY GROUPS

**Practice Targets:** Readiness, Descriptors, Discourse
**Level:** ☆ (can be adapted to various levels)
**Group Size:** Small
**Repeat:** Yes
**Materials:** Copies of the *Story Group Scenes*
**Preparation:** Copy enough of the *Story Group Scenes* so that each student has one scene. Cut out each scene, keeping them with the correct story. (Helpful hints: Copy each story onto different colors of paper.)

### ACTIVITY 1   SETTING THE SCENE

**Directions:** This pantomime activity uses the *Story Group Scenes* on the following pages. Notice that the stories have 3, 4 or 5 scenes. Assign students to groups according to the number of scenes in the stories. For example, the group receiving *The Ice Cream* story should have four people. Together they will determine the correct sequence of the scenes.

Assign students to their Story Groups. Distribute a scene from the story to each person in the group and explain that they are not to share the written scene with anyone in the group. Instruct students to individually develop a pantomime of their scene.

When the group is ready each member will pantomime their scene. Together the group will determine the order of the scenes, practice the story by putting the pantomimes together and later perform the story for the class.

### ACTIVITY 2   TELLING A STORY

**Directions:** Pair students. Using the stories with the scenes in order, instruct one of the partners to assume the role of a narrator. The narrator will sign the story while the other partner pantomimes the actions.

### ACTIVITY 3   STORY EXTENSIONS

**Materials:** The first scene card from each story.

**Directions:** Assign students to small groups of 5 or 6. Distribute the first scene of a story to one of the group members. Ask that student to pantomime the action on the card. Instruct the next student to pantomime something that could happen next. The third student should pantomime another thing that could happen. The remaining students in the group should continue to add to the story with pantomime.

23

# BULL'S EYE

A unique story should develop. Student groups can refine and practice their stories to perform for the class.

## ACTIVITY 4   RIGHT SCENE, WRONG STORY
(For this activity you will want story scenes on the same color of paper.)

**Directions:** For more advanced students, randomly distribute all of the story scenes to the students. Do not worry about arranging the students into story groups however, if students have more than one scene make sure that their scenes originate from the same story. Instruct students to develop pantomime skits for their scene/s.

When students are ready they will try to locate their story group by pantomiming their scenes for each other. This can be done as a group or by bringing up students one by one to the front of the room.

# BULL'S EYE

## *STORY GROUP SCENES*

**THE ICE CREAM**

Walk into the grocery store and find a cart. The first cart is stuck. Put your foot up to try to separate the carts. Try a few different carts. They're all stuck. Finally make one last strong attempt and separate the carts.

Push your grocery cart immediately to the ice cream aisle. Stand with the freezer door open and spend some time deciding on just the right brand of ice cream. Put the half gallon of ice cream in the baby seat of the cart. Then head down several more aisles filling up your cart. Choose meat and check the freshness. Choose a mellon in the vegetable department. Get two gallons of milk. Get enough items that your cart becomes very heavy to push.

You are pushing your full grocery cart through the last aisle toward the check out stand. Look at the ice cream you put in the baby seat of the grocery cart. It is beginning to melt. Scrape up some of the drips with a tissue from your pocket. As you hurry towards the check out stand you notice a friend you haven't seen since last year. Surprised and excited head over to your friend at the end of a very long but crowded aisle. Try to get her attention. She does not see you. Try two different ways to get her to notice you but you. You are still unsuccessful. Frustrated, look at your ice cream once more. It is still melting. Wipe it up again.

You have been trying to get the attention of a friend who you have not seen since last year. You tried two different ways to get her attention and now you simply yell at her across the store. (Remember it's a pantomime yell...) You are successful and both of you push your carts toward each other. You remember that your ice cream is melting. Wipe it up with your sleeve. Continue to talk for a bit and then unload your groceries. As you unload the ice cream you notice that it is now all over the floor!

25

THIS PAGE REPRODUCIBLE FOR CLASSROOM USE ONLY.

# BULL'S EYE

## *STORY GROUP SCENES*

**THE FIRE**

> You are visiting a cabin in the woods. You are now searching for wood but it is scarce. It is getting late and cold. Look everywhere you can to find enough for an armful. Bring it back to the cabin and place it at the back door. Walk into the cabin and shut the door.

> You are visiting a cabin in the woods. You are cold. It is time to build a fire. Open the back door and bring the small pile of stacked wood to the fireplace. Kneel by the fireplace. Find some newspaper, crumple it and place the pieces in the fireplace. Arrange the wood meticulously over the newspaper. Make the perfect fire.

> You are visiting a cabin in the woods and are in the process of building a fire. You are meticulous about the way you arrange the wood. Kneeling by the fireplace, place the last couple of pieces on the fire. Sit back and admire your work. It is still cold. Check one of your pockets for matches. They are not there. Check another pocket. No luck. Check all your pockets, each one a bit more frantically. Stand up and check all around the cabin for matches. Shivering, look everywhere.

> You are visiting a cabin in the woods and have built the perfect fire. Shivering, you have been searching your pockets for matches. You have also searched the cabin without luck. Sit down by the fireplace and shiver. As you look out the window you see someone walking by. Run out and ask her for a match. When she gives you one, run back into the house and light the fire. Look satisfied as you sit back and enjoy the warmth.

# BULL'S EYE

## *STORY GROUP SCENES*

**THE POT**

> Open the old wooden door to your potting shed. Pull out several different sizes, looking for just the perfect pot for your plant. Pantomime several different shapes and sizes. Find three very large pots which satisfy you and place them on the ground. Admire them and return the rest of the pots to the shed.

> Close the old wooden door to your potting shed. Take the three large pots to your dirt pile in the corner of the yard. Return to the shed and take out your shovel. In the hot sun, break up the dirt clods and dig deeply in the dirt pile to find the best dirt. Fill the large pots with soil. Try lifting each of the pots. They are too heavy. With a frustrated face, lean on your shovel and think a minute. Look as though you have just thought of an idea and hurry off to the patio and get the little red wagon. Look satisfied.

> One by one, load three very heavy clay pots onto your little red wagon in the very hot sun. With a great deal of effort, pull your little red wagon filled with pots up the hill in your yard. Struggle with each of the pots as you take them out of the wagon and place them on your front step.

> You are ready to plant some seeds in the pots you filled. Pull out several different seed packets from your pocket and choose the ones you want to plant. Poke several little holes in each of the pots. Rip open the packets and put the seeds in the soil. Carefully move the soil to cover the seeds.

> You have just planted flower seeds in some very heavy pots. The sun is hot, the work was hard and the pots were heavy. On your knees near the pot, check the seeds you just covered with soil. Go to the potting shed and find your watering can. Find the outdoor water spigot and fill the can. Water your flowers carefully. Move the pots one last time to get them into just the perfect place on your porch. Stand back and look satisfied with a job well done.

# BULL'S EYE

## STORY GROUP SCENES

**THE BABY**

> On your way past the family room in your home, notice the screaming baby. Look around the hall for the parents. Nervously walk over to the baby. Try to entertain the baby with faces and little tickles. The baby is still inconsolable so try various techniques. Begin to show some frustration as you pick up the baby. Take the baby into the hall and look for someone to take the baby. Notice the baby's Grandmother in the next room. Hand the baby over to Grandma quickly and take off.

> You are the Grandmother of a screaming baby. You were rocking in the other room when someone just handed the baby to you. The baby is screaming, red-faced and inconsolable and you are quite surprised to have this squirming, noisy bundle in your arms. As a Grandmother though, you have had lots of experience with comforting babies. Find the rocking chair and with all your serenity and patience, gently rock the baby. When she is quiet, you both fall asleep.

> You are walking down the hall of a house when you look into a room and notice a Grandmother with a baby in her arms. Both of them are sleeping in a rocking chair. As you walk by you also notice the really bad smell emanating from the room. Gently pick up the baby without waking Grandma. It is obvious that the baby needs to be changed but the smell is so awful. You are also nervous because you have not changed many diapers in your time. Look nervous as you take the baby from Grandma. After you have the baby in your arms, lay her down on the floor and try to figure out how to change the diaper.

> Walking by a room in a house you notice a Grandmother sleeping in a rocking chair and an inexperienced person trying to change a very stinky diaper on a baby. You are an experienced diaper-changer. Stand by and watch the attempt, smiling. When the person needs help, step in and demonstrate how an expert changes a diaper. When you are finished, return the baby to her room and lay her down for a nap.

# BULL'S EYE

## STORY GROUP SCENES

**THE PEACH**

> Admire a large juicy peach high in a tree. It looks delicious and you are very hungry. Try to reach for it. It is too high. Try to jump for it. Still too high. Try to climb the tree. It is too fragile and the branches bend. Frustrated, stand by the tree and look up at the peach. As you look, a great idea comes to you. Go get your ladder and come back with it. Lean it up against the tree.

> You are hungry for a peach you see high in a tree. You have your ladder leaning up against the tree. Position the ladder carefully. Check the footing and the balance. Carefully, climb up the ladder all the way to the top. Reach out for the peach. It is still too high. Stretch your arm out even farther and stand carefully on the tips of your toes. Try this a few times, each time, missing the peach. Frustrated, descend the ladder.

> You are hungry for a peach you see high in a tree. You have your ladder leaning up against the tree. You are frustrated because even with the ladder you cannot reach the peach. Move the ladder to a better place so that you can reach the peach easier. Climb back up the ladder and hoist yourself up on a limb. Stretch out and reach the peach. Watch your feet as the ladder slips and falls to the ground. Stuck on the limb you realize that you have to let go and drop to the ground. Put the peach in your back pocket. Drop to the ground, falling on your behind. Stand up and try to dig out the squashed peach from your pocket.

# BULL'S EYE

## *STORY GROUP SCENES*

**THE SUITCASE**

> You are preparing for a vacation. Walk down the stairs in your home and open the door to the storage room. It is full of cobwebs and dust. Push the webs away, cough and start moving stuff out of the way. Your suitcase is in the back of the room with lots of stuff between you

> You are preparing for a vacation and are in the storage room in your home. Happily you spot your suitcase and move the last bit of stuff out of the way. Pull out your suitcase, sit it on the floor and dust it off. Sneeze and wipe your brow. It's been hard work.

> Tired and full of cobwebs, you are sitting on your suitcase in the hall of your home. Finish your rest and bring the suitcase upstairs to your bedroom. Toss it on the bed and begin pulling clothes from your drawers and closet. Identify the clothes as you put them in. When you are satisfied that you have enough clothes and the suitcase is piled high with your things, try to close it. You are unsuccessful.

> You are trying to close your very full suitcase. The clothes are piled too high. Take a couple of items out of the suitcase, identify them and think about putting them away. Change your mind. You may need them. Return to the suitcase and rearrange several of the items. Try to close it again. No luck. Sit on the suitcase as a last resort. Try to close the suitcase now. Success!

 **BULL'S EYE**

## AND WHO ARE YOU?

**Practice Targets:** Readiness, Structures, Discourse, Articulation
**Level:** ★★
**Group Size:** Large
**Repeat:** Yes
**Materials:** *And Who Are You* copied pages, note cards, masking tape
**Preparation:** Copy the page in the Teacher's Manual and cut out each name. Mount them on note cards and laminate.

**Directions:** The object of this game is for students to figure out, by asking Yes/No questions to various classmates, the name on the note card taped to their backs.

Distribute a notecard to each student. Instruct students to tape that card onto a classmate's back without revealing the name on the card. When each student has a *new identity*, instruct them to mill around the room and try to figure out the name on their backs. Students are restricted to asking Yes/No questions and answering with either a "Yes" or a "No."

If students seem reluctant or confused, encourage them to ask questions
like:   "Am I...living    ...dead        ...young         ...old

　　　　...woman      ...man         ...boy           ...girl

　　　...T.V. character   ...animal    ...movie character   ...human    etc.

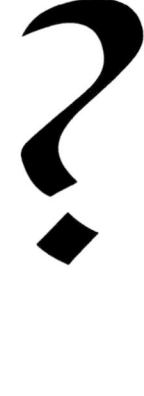

# BULL'S EYE

## *AND WHO ARE YOU?*
### IDENTITY CARDS

| | | | |
|---|---|---|---|
| CLYDE DREXLER | PRINCE CHARLES | EINSTEIN | ELMER FUDD |
| SNOOPY | ROMEO | BOB MARLEY | PAUL BUNYON |
| MR. T | BILL COSBY | BACH | FLOUNDER |
| JENNY CRAIG | ARIEL | THOMAS EDISON | BUGS BUNNY |
| DRACULA | ABRAHAM LINCOLN | CAPTAIN KANGAROO | RANDY TRAVIS |
| PAULA ABDUL | ERNIE | FRANK ZAPPA | QUEEN ELIZABETH |
| LINDA BOVE | MADONNA | DONNY OSMOND | MINNIE MOUSE |

## BULL'S EYE

## AND WHO ARE YOU?
### IDENTITY CARDS

| YOGI BEAR | PETER PAN | BAMBI | CAPTAIN HOOK |
|---|---|---|---|
| SNOW WHITE | BEETHOVEN | WOLF MAN | PINK PANTHER |
| SALLY FIELD | DATA | FLIPPER | POCAHONTAS |
| BILL CLINTON | I. KING JORDAN | KENNY ROGERS | MARLEE MATLIN |
| KEVIN COSTNER | TOM CRUISE | NOLAN RYAN | SADDAAM HUSSEIN |
| GARTH BROOKS | MARILYN MONROE | SPEEDY GONZALEZ | PETER BRADY |
| JULIA ROBERTS | KEANU REEVES | GOLDIE HAWN | GEORGE WASHINGTON |

# BULL'S EYE

## *AND WHO ARE YOU?*
### IDENTITY CARDS

| CASPER | BATMAN | KELLY MCGILLIS | GHANDI |
|---|---|---|---|
| WHOOPI GOLDBERG | WENDY DARLING | FRED FLINTSTONE | BURT REYNOLDS |
| MEL GIBSON | MICHAEL JACKSON | KING ARTHUR | JERRY GARCIA |
| RICHIE RICH | BLONDIE | LYLE LOVETT | BARBARA STREISAND |
| LUCILLE BALL | AMELIA EHRHART | PRINCESS DI | YOUR PRINCIPAL |
|  |  |  |  |
|  |  |  |  |

 # BULL'S EYE

## DEVELOP A SURVEY

**Practice Targets:** Readiness, Structures, Discourse, Articulation
**Level:** ★★
**Group Size:** Large
**Repeat:** Yes, Twice
**Materials:** Student Workbook pages 11, 12, 13, pencil
**Preparation:** Arrange an area in the room where students can mill around

**Directions:** There are two surveys in the workbook. Choose the survey the students will use. Instruct students to turn to the Workbook page. Allow time for students to develop one ASL question for each of the pictures on the page. Those questions will become the basis for the student's survey. If students need to record their questions, encourage them to write short notes or draw pictures instead of writing full English sentences.

When ready, each student will individually interview five classmates using the same questions. The names of the classmates can be recorded at the top of the Workbook page. Students can record the answers to their survey questions on the Workbook page.

Encourage students to use their creativity to consider different question ideas before they decide on one. For example, the following questions could be asked using their ASL equivalent. "When was the last time you got a present?, What was the worst gift you ever received?, When is your birthday?, How many gifts do you typically buy at Christmas?, What would be the perfect gift for you?"

Each student should have a completed survey at the end of this activity. Convene as a large group and discuss the survey questions and answers.

# BULL'S EYE

## DEVELOP A SURVEY

REPLICAS OF *DEVELOP A SURVEY* FROM STUDENT WORKBOOK - PAGES 12, 13

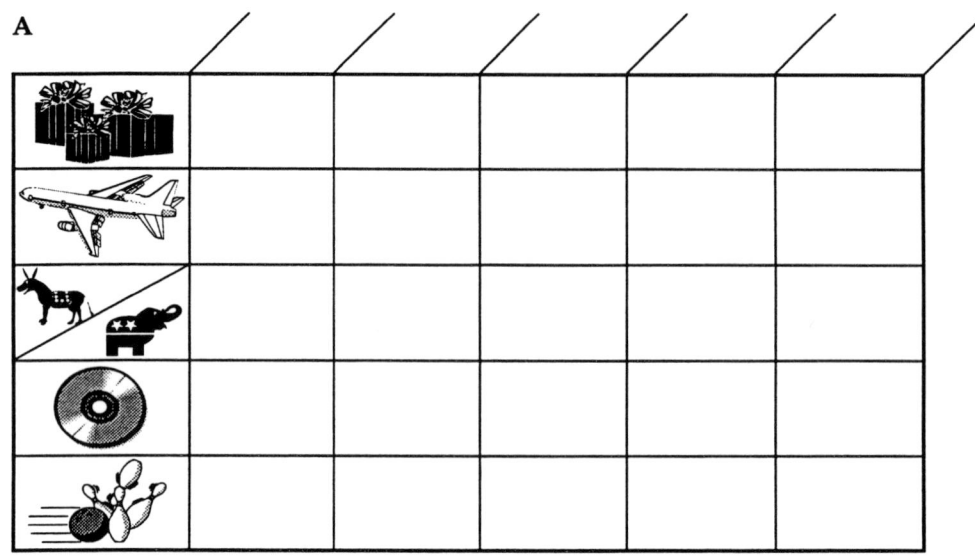

36

 **BULL'S EYE**

## *NOW YOU SEE IT, NOW YOU DON'T*

**Practice Targets:** Readiness, Descriptors, Structures, Articulation
**Level:** ★★
**Group Size:** Small
**Repeat:** Yes
**Materials:** Numerous common household and school objects, trays, cloths to cover each tray, paper and pencil for each student pair
**Preparation:** Prepare a tray of approximately 10-20 common objects for each four to six students in the class. Cover each tray with a cloth.

The object of this activity is to memorize and record by drawing, the most correct number of items on the tray in their correct location.

Directions: Pair students and then assign each pair to one or two other pairs, creating groups of 4 - 6. Give each group a covered tray. Explain that students will have 1 minute to memorize the objects on the tray and their locations.

Watch the clock for 1 minute. When time is up, each pair of students will work together to draw the items and the tray. One partner will begin by describing one item and its location on the tray. The other partner will draw that description on paper. Partners will take turns describing the items and drawing. Encourage students to use gestures, any signs they know, classifiers, and fingerspelling. It is imperative however, that one partner describe an item while the other partner draws it. A partner cannot simply draw the location of one of the items.

# BULL'S EYE

## NOW YOU SEE IT, NOW YOU DON'T
### OBJECT IDEAS

| tape | silverware | rubber band | pen | match stick |
|---|---|---|---|---|
| CD | stick of gum | paper clip | pink eraser | chalk |
| spatula | balloon | perfume | rock/shell | white-out |
| candle | dice | toothbrush | safety pin | ruler |
| coffee cup | spice jar | salt shaker | stick or leaf | stationery |
| small book | jar top | lollipop | tweezers | floppy disk |
| video tape | straw | pine cone | scissors | muffin mix |
| necklace | calculator | ball | sticky notes | can of food |
| lunch bag | receipt | pill box | turkey baster | whisk |

# BULL'S EYE

## WHAT'S INSIDE?

**Practice Targets:** Readiness, Discourse, Articulation
**Level:** ★★
**Group Size:** Small
**Repeat:** Yes
**Materials:** Paper and pencil for each team
**Preparation:** None

The object of this activity is to generate the longest list of unduplicated objects that might be found in each container.

**Directions:** Assign students to small groups. Designate one team member to become the "recorder" for the group.

Choose one of the containers listed below. Write it on the board. Inform small groups that they will have three minutes to compile a list of objects that might be found in the container. Students may use finerspelling or signs that they know.

When time is up reconvene as a class. Groups can compare their lists. Eliminate duplicate items. The group with the longest list of objects wins the game.

## CONTAINERS

| COAT POCKET | DESK DRAWER | BRIEFCASE | LARGE ENVELOPE |
| --- | --- | --- | --- |
| GLOVE COMPARTMENT | PURSE | GYM BAG | SCHOOL LOCKER |
| DRYER VENT | SUITCASE | TRUNK | BACKPACK |
| TOOL BOX | CLOSET | HOPE CHEST | CHILD'S DESK |

**Example: COAT POCKET**
1. Change
2. Keys
3. Cigarettes
4. Lint
5. Bus pass
6. Wallet
7. Rabbit's foot
8. Address book
9. Gum
10. Breath mints
11. Receipt
12. Business card

# BULL'S EYE

## CATEGORIES

**Practice Targets:** Structures, Discourse, Articulation
**Level:** ★★
**Group Size:** Large or small
**Repeat:** Yes
**Materials:** *Category list*
**Preparation:** None

The object of this activity is to be the first person to figure out the criteria that links all of the described items together.

**Directions:** Choose one of the categories from the list on the following page. Begin by signing or describing one item that fits into the category you have chosen. After each item pause to give students time to think about the items and make connections. During the pause students can ask Yes/No questions such as the ASL equivalent of "Will ____ fit into the category?" The use of Yes/No questions will enable students to figure out how the items are connected. The student who correctly guesses the category will have the opportunity to select another category and present it to the class.

**Example: Short things**
Sign the ASL equivalent of: "A bush fits into this category, A child fits into this category, A coffee table fits into this category." Etc. Continue until a student correctly guesses the category of short things.

**Category: Things in a kitchen**

**Note: this activity works well in review of the concept of Existential Have.**

Sign the ASL equivalent of:
There is milk in the category.
There is a light in the category.

There are cups in the category.
There is a door in the category.

# BULL'S EYE

## CATEGORIES

| Things that grow | Oriental things | Things in a medicine cabinet | Wooden things |
|---|---|---|---|
| Old fashioned things | Things at a circus | Plastic things | Sports things |
| Things in a desert | Board games | Things with wheels | Things on a farm |
| Things that float | Square things | Things at a funeral parlor | Things that sink |
| Things at a police station | Paper things | College things | Things in a garage |
| Tall things | Things on a boat | Baby things | Brass things |
| Camping things | Things at a plumbing store | Expensive things | Bathroom things |
| Things at a dry cleaner's | Soft things | Garden things | Things in a pet store |
| Teacher things | Party things | Things in a potting shed | Things in a garage |

41

# BULL'S EYE

## WHO OWNS THE GALLERY?

**Practice Targets:** Descriptors, Structures, Discourse, Articulation
**Level:** ★★
**Group Size:** Pairs
**Repeat:** Yes (limited)
**Materials:** Student Workbook pages 14, 15, 16, pencil
**Preparation:** None

**Background Information:** A scout for a movie mogul is looking for the perfect location for the mogul's next film. He is meeting with a local real estate agent who knows the owners of all of the buildings in the city of Hampton. The scout wishes to obtain permission from each of the owners of the buildings to allow film crews to film in each building. To do so the scout must first determine who owns each of the buildings.

### ACTIVITY 1    TEACHER/REALTOR

The object of this activity is for the students to discover, by using Yes/No questions, the owners of the buildings in Hampton.

**Directions:** Inform students that you will assume the role of the Realtor. The entire class will play the part of the movie scout. Privately assign owners to each of the buildings on the example on the following page.

Explain that students will need to develop Yes/No questions in order to find out the identities of the building owners. For example, a student could ask the ASL equivalent of "Does Mr. Shultz own the bank?" You would respond with the ASL equivalent of, "No, Mr. Shultz does not own the bank."

Students will take turns asking Yes/No questions. Instruct students to record the names of the owners on the first line below each building on the Workbook page. Through the process of elimination, students will discover the identities of the building owners.

# BULL'S EYE

## ACTIVITY 2   ON YOUR OWN

**Directions:** Pair students. Select one partner to assume the role of the Realtor. Instruct the Realtor to privately assign owner names to each of the buildings and record them on the second line under each of the buildings. Inform the other student that he will become the scout.

The scout can begin the activity by forming Yes/No questions in an effort to discover the names of the owners. Remind the Realtor that he must answer the scout's questions with complete ASL sentences.

When the scout has figured out all of the building owners, the partners will switch roles. The third line under the buildings will be used to record the names.

## REPLICA OF *WHO'S OWNS THE GALLERY?* FROM STUDENT WORKBOOK - PAGE 16

Owners' names: Mr. Alsdurf, Ms. Flannery, Mr. Shultz, Ms. Novotny, Ms. Mc Greevy, Ms. Rice, Mr. Rolling, Mr. Wagner, Ms. Flynn, Mrs. O'Cell, Mr. Henry

Kiddie Kare   "Inn at the Top"   Retirement Center   Instant Insurance

Planetarium   Bank   Funny Farms   Alsdurf Gallery

# BULL'S EYE

## JEN AND MAGGIE'S SCHEDULE

**Practice Targets:** Time, Numerals, Discourse, Articulation
**Level:** ★★
**Group Size:** Pairs
**Repeat:** No
**Materials:** Student Workbook pages 17, 18, pencil
**Preparation:** None

**Background Information:** Jen and Maggie are twins. Partners have been hired to become the "nannies" for these twins. The previous nannies departed unexpectedly and left no schedules for the girls. This activity represents the first meeting of the nannies, who were hired separately.

**Directions:** Pair students. Assign a nanny to Jen and a nanny to Maggie. Each nanny will privately record a daily schedule for their twin on the Workbook page. Jen's nanny will describe his twin's schedule. Maggie's nanny will record that schedule on the Workbook page. Then Maggie's nanny will describe his twin's schedule while Jen's nanny records it.

When the Workbook pages are complete, students can compare their completed schedules. Workbook pages for each pair should be identical.

## REPLICA OF *JEN AND MAGGIE'S SCHEDULE* FROM STUDENT WORKBOOK - PAGE 18

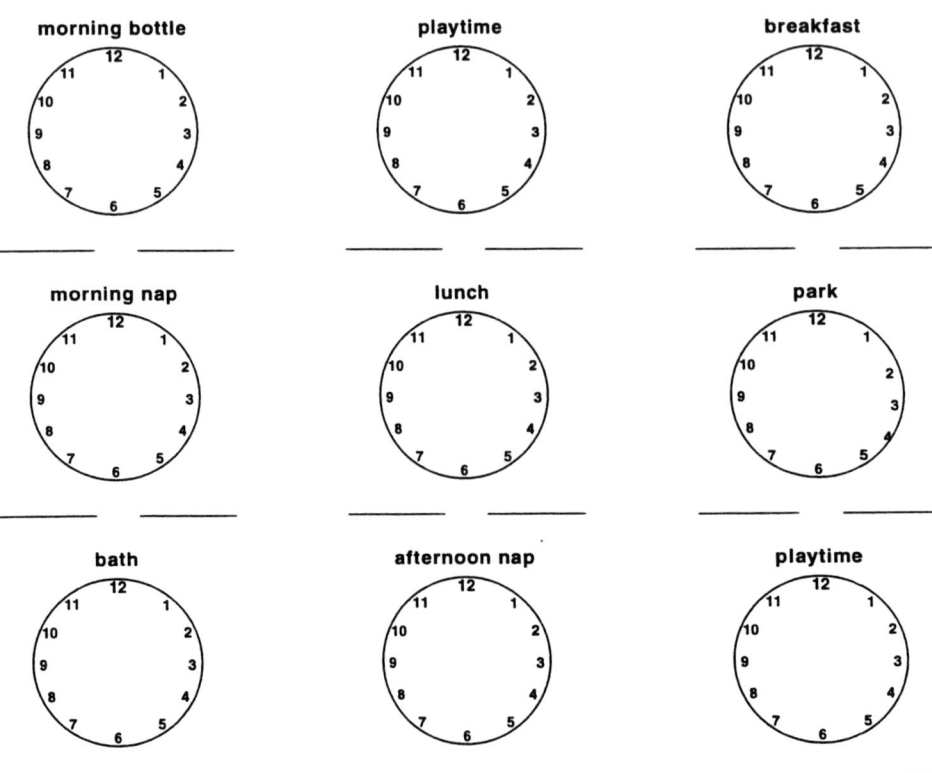

# BULL'S EYE

## OUTPATIENT CLINICS

**Practice Targets:** Numerals, Time, Discourse, Structures, Articulation
**Level:** ★★
**Group Size:** Pairs
**Repeat:** No
**Materials:** Student Workbook pages 19, 20, pencil
**Preparation:** None

**Background Information:** Students will assume the roles of hospital administrators in neighboring small counties. The mayors of both communities are eager for the two hospitals to make an effort to increase the availability of outpatient clinic days for the Hampton/Northfield area. For example, the allergy clinic at the Hampton Hospital is open on the same day as the allergy clinic at Northfield General Hospital. There are several duplicated clinic days. In an effort to provide better service, the hospital administrators are meeting to design their clinic schedules without duplication.

**Directions:** Pair students. Assign one student the role of the Hampton Hospital administrator and the other student to the role of the administrator of the Northfield General Hospital. Instruct administrators to privately create a clinic schedule using the options listed on the Workbook page. Each administrator will determine whether a specific clinic will be open daily, weekly, bi-weekly or monthly and then decide which day or days of the week patients can be seen. Each option must be used at least once in the schedule. Schedules should be recorded on the appropriate line on the Workbook page under each specialty.

Each administrator will take a turn and describe his outpatient schedule while his partner records it on the appropriate line on the Workbook page.

After both outpatient clinic schedules have been recorded, administrators will discuss any duplication of services, and balance of clinic days. Together they will create a final schedule using the third line of the Workbook page that is guaranteed to please the both communities.

**Hampton Hospital**
*Serving you since 1914*

**Northfield General**
*quality community care*

# BULL'S EYE

## *OUTPATIENT CLINICS*

**REPLICA OF *OUTPATIENT CLINICS* FROM STUDENT WORKBOOK - PAGE 20**

**Hampton Hospital**
*serving you since 1914*
**OUTPATIENT CLINICS**

**Northfield General**
*quality community care*
**OUTPATIENT CLINICS**

| Hampton Hospital | | Northfield General | |
|---|---|---|---|
| *ALLERGY* | *NEUROLOGY* | *ALLERGY* | *NEUROLOGY* |
| *PULMINARY* | *ONCOLOGY* | *PULMINARY* | *ONCOLOGY* |
| *GYNECOLOGY* | *SURGERY* | *GYNECOLOGY* | *SURGERY* |
| *UROLOGY* | *ORTHOPEDICS* | *UROLOGY* | *ORTHOPEDICS* |

OPTIONS: MONDAYS, TUESDAYS, WEDNESDAYS, THURSDAYS, FRIDAYS, SATURDAYS
OPTIONS: DAILY, WEEKLY, BI-WEEKLY, MONTHLY

# BULL'S EYE

## DAYRUNNING

**Practice Targets:** Time, Numerals, Discourse, Structures, Articulation
**Level:** ★★★
**Group Size:** Pairs
**Repeat:** No
**Materials:** Copies of Dayrunning Schedules pages 48 - 52 in Teacher's Manual, pencil
**Preparation:** None

**Note:** There are three different schedules in the Workbook which apply to these directions. The object of each activity is to find a mutually agreeable time for the pair to meet. The first two sets of schedules are complete. The third set is blank.

**Directions:** Pair students. Determine which activity you will use. Assign each student to one of the roles. (Warden/Security Instructor, School Superintendent/Urban Planner, Energy Salesman/Director of Nuclear Waste Treatment).

Inform students that they must find a mutually agreeable time to meet with each other without rescheduling or canceling an activity or appointment. If one partner cannot meet, the other partner should record the conflicting activity on his Workbook page.

**Example (partners will sign the ASL equivalent of:)**
    PARTNER 1:  "Are you busy Monday morning at 8:30?"
    PARTNER 2:  "Yes. I have a dentist appointment until 9:30. What about Monday morning
                    at 10:00?"
    PARTNER 1:  "You're busy with the dentist from 8:30-10:00. I am unavailable at 10:00. I am
                    meeting with Meredith's teacher until 10:45. Can you meet at 11:00?"

Conversation continues in this manner until partners have found a meeting time and recorded all the conflicts in their schedules.

**Hint:** To avoid the opportunity to simply look at a partner's schedule, arrange students so that partners are seated at some distance from each other in a large circle.

# BULL'S EYE

## JADE COUNTY JAIL
*here the inmates are green with envy*

### WARDEN'S DAILY CALENDAR

**Monday**
- 8:00
- 9:00
- 10:00
- 11:00 PAROLE BOARD MEETING
- 12:00
- 1:00
- 2:00
- 3:00
- 4:00 KARATE
- 5:00

**Tuesday**
- 8:00
- 9:00 OFFICE WORK
- 10:00
- 11:00
- 12:00
- 1:00
- 2:00 LUNCH W/ GOVERNOR
- 3:00
- 4:00
- 5:00

**Wednesday**
- 8:00 BREAKFAST MEETING
- 9:00
- 10:00
- 11:00 PAROLE BOARD MEETING
- 12:00
- 1:00
- 2:00 OFFICE WORK
- 3:00
- 4:00
- 5:00

**Thursday**
- 8:00 DENTIST
- 9:00
- 10:00 TARGET PRACTICE
- 11:00
- 12:00 LUNCH WITH DISTRICT ATTORNEY
- 1:00 LUNCH - MARIAN HARPER
- 2:00 REVIEW FILES
- 3:00 PREPARE FOR AUDIT
- 4:00
- 5:00 KARATE

**Friday**
- 8:00 COUNSELING
- 9:00 MEET WITH INMATES
- 10:00 COUNCIL MEETING
- 11:00
- 12:00
- 1:00
- 2:00 FOOD SERVICE MEETING
- 3:00
- 4:00
- 5:00

# BULL'S EYE

## COMMUNITY COLLEGE CAMPUS SECURITY

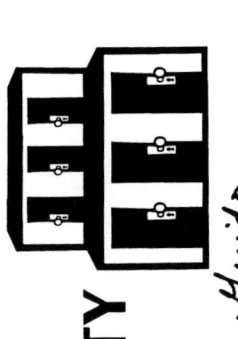

*we'll get your dorm back to norm*

### planning calendar

**Monday**
- 8:00 Welcome - Training Class
- 9:00 Goals & Objectives
- 10:00 Student Trainee responsibilities
- 11:00
- 12:00 Campus phone system
- 1:00 Lunch with Hugo
- 2:00 Tour of campus
- 3:00 Library explanation
- 4:00
- 5:00

**Tuesday**
- 8:00 Lecture
- 9:00 Guest lecture (Lon Gunn)
- 10:00 CCCS Rules
- 11:00 Procedures lecture
- 12:00 Policies lecture
- 1:00 Lunch - (find lecturer)
- 2:00
- 3:00
- 4:00 Safety Demonstration
- 5:00 (continued)

**Wednesday**
- 8:00
- 9:00 Sexual Harassment - Part I
- 10:00
- 11:00
- 12:00 Sexual Harassment - Part II
- 1:00 Lunch - Lore Maybone - speaker "Valuing Diversity"
- 2:00
- 3:00
- 4:00
- 5:00

**Thursday**
- 8:00
- 9:00 Lecture on proper restraint
- 10:00
- 11:00
- 12:00
- 1:00
- 2:00
- 3:00
- 4:00
- 5:00

**Friday**
- 8:00
- 9:00
- 10:00
- 11:00 Proper restraint Practice
- 12:00 "
- 1:00
- 2:00
- 3:00 Graduation Ceremonies
- 4:00 "
- 5:00 Cocktails with Lenora

# MARION SCHOOL DISTRICT #337
*serving the needs of all children*

## SUPERINTENDENT'S WEEKLY CALENDAR

**Monday**
- 8:00
- 9:00
- 10:00
- 11:00 PTA council meeting
- 12:00 At-risk luncheon
- 1:00 office work
- 2:00 "
- 3:00
- 4:00
- 5:00

**Tuesday**
- 8:00
- 9:00 site-based management
- 10:00 committee meeting
- 11:00
- 12:00
- 1:00
- 2:00
- 3:00 meet with food service reps.
- 4:00 " "
- 5:00

**Wednesday**
- 8:00
- 9:00
- 10:00
- 11:00 prepare for speech
- 12:00 principals' luncheon
- 1:00
- 2:00
- 3:00 meeting with district accountant
- 4:00 Don Halstad - meeting
- 5:00

**Thursday**
- 8:00 on-site visitations
- 9:00
- 10:00
- 11:00
- 12:00
- 1:00
- 2:00
- 3:00 closing of Flannery Fairway - speech
- 4:00
- 5:00 cocktails with Muncie Superintendent

**Friday**
- 8:00
- 9:00 meeting with mayor
- 10:00 Administrators' meeting
- 11:00
- 12:00
- 1:00 Renovation team meeting
- 2:00
- 3:00
- 4:00
- 5:00

# CITY SCAPES

**urban planning specialists**

**let us plan your urban sprawl**

**weekly calendar**

**Monday**
- 8:00 realtor's "walkabout"
- 9:00 ⟨
- 10:00 ⟨
- 11:00
- 12:00
- 1:00
- 2:00
- 3:00 show apartment building
- 4:00 Mall Grand Opening
- 5:00

**Tuesday**
- 8:00 Breakfast with Annie
- 9:00
- 10:00
- 11:00 Better Business Bureau Mtg.
- 12:00
- 1:00 Appraisal of Brentwood Apts.
- 2:00
- 3:00
- 4:00
- 5:00

**Wednesday**
- 8:00 Hospital Auxillary Breakfast
- 9:00 ⟨
- 10:00 ⟨
- 11:00
- 12:00
- 1:00 show Chamber's home
- 2:00 show Stevenson's dump
- 3:00
- 4:00
- 5:00 Naturopath appt.

**Thursday**
- 8:00
- 9:00
- 10:00
- 11:00
- 12:00
- 1:00 Integrated selling class
- 2:00 ⟨
- 3:00
- 4:00 Golf with Richard Poorer
- 5:00

**Friday**
- 8:00 Breakfast with William Stover
- 9:00
- 10:00
- 11:00 New trainee arrives
- 12:00
- 1:00
- 2:00
- 3:00
- 4:00 show Nash Mansion
- 5:00 Cocktails with Lotta Cash

# BULL'S EYE

# NUCLEAR WASTE DISPOSAL
## we'll glow on you

**Monday**
- 8:00 _____
- 9:00 _____
- 10:00 _____
- 11:00 _____
- 12:00 _____
- 1:00 _____
- 2:00 _____
- 3:00 _____
- 4:00 _____
- 5:00 _____

**Tuesday**
- 8:00 _____
- 9:00 _____
- 10:00 _____
- 11:00 _____
- 12:00 _____
- 1:00 _____
- 2:00 _____
- 3:00 _____
- 4:00 _____
- 5:00 _____

**Wednesday**
- 8:00 _____
- 9:00 _____
- 10:00 _____
- 11:00 _____
- 12:00 _____
- 1:00 _____
- 2:00 _____
- 3:00 _____
- 4:00 _____
- 5:00 _____

**Thursday**
- 8:00 _____
- 9:00 _____
- 10:00 _____
- 11:00 _____
- 12:00 _____
- 1:00 _____
- 2:00 _____
- 3:00 _____
- 4:00 _____
- 5:00 _____

**Friday**
- 8:00 _____
- 9:00 _____
- 10:00 _____
- 11:00 _____
- 12:00 _____
- 1:00 _____
- 2:00 _____
- 3:00 _____
- 4:00 _____
- 5:00 _____

# BULL'S EYE

## AMERICAN ENERGY SUPPLY COMPANY

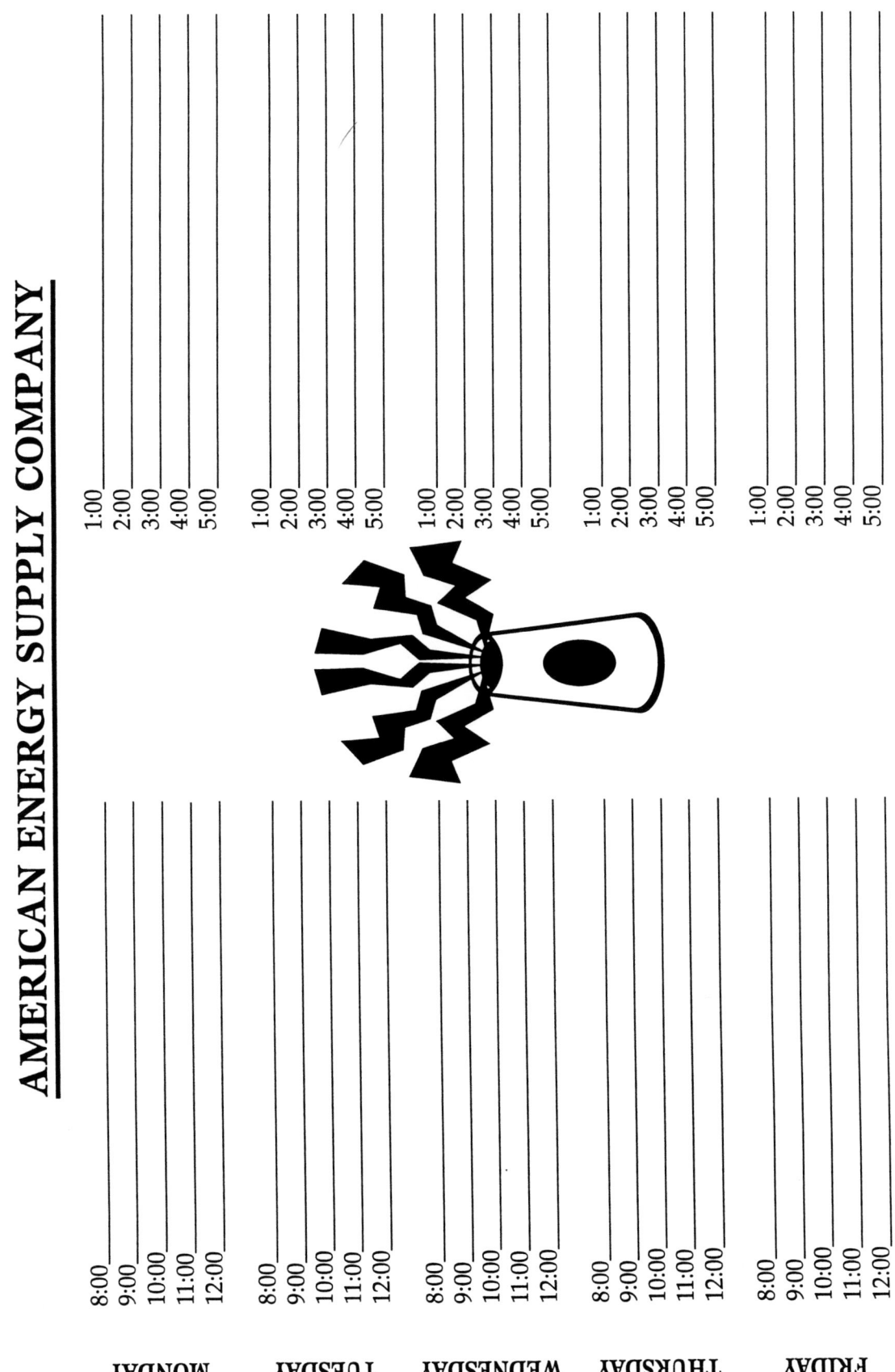

|        | 8:00 | 9:00 | 10:00 | 11:00 | 12:00 | 1:00 | 2:00 | 3:00 | 4:00 | 5:00 |
|--------|------|------|-------|-------|-------|------|------|------|------|------|
| MONDAY    | | | | | | | | | | |
| TUESDAY   | | | | | | | | | | |
| WEDNESDAY | | | | | | | | | | |
| THURSDAY  | | | | | | | | | | |
| FRIDAY    | | | | | | | | | | |

# BULL'S EYE

## *KIDDIE KARE FINGERPAINTING "FAUX PAS"*

**Practice Targets:** Numerals, Discourse, Structures, Time, Articulation
**Level:** ★★
**Group Size:** Small
**Repeat:** No
**Materials:** Student Workbook pages 21, 22, pencil
**Preparation:** None

**Background Information:** Students are members of the staff of the Kiddie Kare Day Care Center, a licensed facility for children from birth to five years. While the supervisor was away yesterday little Christopher snuck into the office and fingerpainted on many of the recent records of the childrens' activities. Since the supervisor needs those documents for a meeting tonight the staff members have gathered to recreate those records.

**Directions:** Assign students to small groups of three. Assign three children to each group member. Instruct students to privately create activities that each of their children have done, focusing on things that might have happened last month, last week, yesterday and today. The activities should be recorded on the Workbook page using notes or drawings.

Each small group will meet. One by one, members will sign the ASL equivalent of the information he recorded about his three children. The remaining group members will record that information on the Workbook page by drawing or making short notes.

Each group can submit their completed documents to the teacher "supervisor" for review. It could be shared with another small group or the entire class.

## REPLICA OF *KIDDIE KARE FINGERPAINTING "FAUX PAS"* FROM STUDENT WORKBOOK - PAGE 22

| Liz | Meredith | Christopher |
|---|---|---|
| last month: _____ | last month: _____ | last month: _____ |
| last week: _____ | last week: _____ | last week: _____ |
| yesterday: _____ | yesterday: _____ | yesterday: _____ |
| today: _____ | today: _____ | today: _____ |

| Matthew | Jessica | Caroline |
|---|---|---|
| last month: _____ | last month: _____ | last month: _____ |
| last week: _____ | last week: _____ | last week: _____ |
| yesterday: _____ | yesterday: _____ | yesterday: _____ |
| today: _____ | today: _____ | today: _____ |

| Gail | David | John |
|---|---|---|
| last month: _____ | last month: _____ | last month: _____ |
| last week: _____ | last week: _____ | last week: _____ |
| yesterday: _____ | yesterday: _____ | yesterday: _____ |
| today: _____ | today: _____ | today: _____ |

# BULL'S EYE

## TWENTY YEAR REUNION

**Practice Targets:** Numerals, Discourse, Structures, Time, Articulation
**Level:** ★★
**Group Size:** Pairs
**Repeat:** No
**Materials:** Student Workbook pages 23, 24, 25, pencil
**Preparation:** None

**Background Information:** Each set of partners is serving on a reunion committee of two. Each partner on the *Missing Persons Committee* has been corresponding with several classmates and knows what has been happening in their lives. Today the two-person committee is meeting to share the information they have gathered over the last few months.

**Directions:** Pair students. Assign a different page to each partner. Partners will look at the pictures of the people and privately create a past, present and future for each of them. Instruct students to draw or write short notes in the boxes on the Workbook page to record where each person lived, their marital status, their occupation and something that they considered an accomplishment at the time. (Their accomplishments do not have to be related to their occupation. Perhaps one of the people ran her first marathon or participated in some silly attempt to break a record!)

Partners will share all of their information with each other and complete their Workbook pages. Workbook pages for each set of partners should have identical information.

# BULL'S EYE

## *TWENTY YEAR REUNION*

REPLICA OF *TWENTY YEAR REUNION* FROM STUDENT WORKBOOK - PAGES 24, 25

**A**

|  | (past)<br>10 year reunion | (present)<br>20 year reunion | (future)<br>40 year reunion |
|---|---|---|---|
| Lori | town: _____<br>married/single: _____<br>occupation: _____<br>accomplishment: _____ | town: _____<br>married/single: _____<br>occupation: _____<br>accomplishment: _____ | town: _____<br>married/single: _____<br>occupation: _____<br>accomplishment: _____ |
| Mike | town: _____<br>married/single: _____<br>occupation: _____<br>accomplishment: _____ | town: _____<br>married/single: _____<br>occupation: _____<br>accomplishment: _____ | town: _____<br>married/single: _____<br>occupation: _____<br>accomplishment: _____ |
| Mary | town: _____<br>married/single: _____<br>occupation: _____<br>accomplishment: _____ | town: _____<br>married/single: _____<br>occupation: _____<br>accomplishment: _____ | town: _____<br>married/single _____<br>occupation: _____<br>accomplishment: _____ |
| Joe | town: _____<br>married/single: _____<br>occupation: _____<br>accomplishment: _____ | town: _____<br>married/single: _____<br>occupation: _____<br>accomplishment: _____ | town: _____<br>married/single: _____<br>occupation: _____<br>accomplishment: _____ |
| Carolyn | town: _____<br>married/single: _____<br>occupation: _____<br>accomplishment: _____ | town: _____<br>married/single: _____<br>occupation: _____<br>accomplishment: _____ | town: _____<br>married/single: _____<br>occupation: _____<br>accomplishment: _____ |

**B**

|  | (past)<br>10 year reunion | (present)<br>20 year reunion | (future)<br>40 year reunion |
|---|---|---|---|
| Bill | town: _____<br>married/single: _____<br>occupation: _____<br>accomplishment: _____ | town: _____<br>married/single: _____<br>occupation: _____<br>accomplishment: _____ | town: _____<br>married/single: _____<br>occupation: _____<br>accomplishment: _____ |
| Doris | town: _____<br>married/single: _____<br>occupation: _____<br>accomplishment: _____ | town: _____<br>married/single: _____<br>occupation: _____<br>accomplishment: _____ | town: _____<br>married/single: _____<br>occupation: _____<br>accomplishment: _____ |
| Steve | town: _____<br>married/single: _____<br>occupation: _____<br>accomplishment: _____ | town: _____<br>married/single: _____<br>occupation: _____<br>accomplishment: _____ | town: _____<br>married/single _____<br>occupation: _____<br>accomplishment: _____ |
| Jack | town: _____<br>married/single: _____<br>occupation: _____<br>accomplishment: _____ | town: _____<br>married/single: _____<br>occupation: _____<br>accomplishment: _____ | town: _____<br>married/single: _____<br>occupation: _____<br>accomplishment: _____ |
| Gretchen | town: _____<br>married/single: _____<br>occupation: _____<br>accomplishment: _____ | town: _____<br>married/single: _____<br>occupation: _____<br>accomplishment: _____ | town: _____<br>married/single: _____<br>occupation: _____<br>accomplishment: _____ |

# BULL'S EYE

## CHORE CHART

**Practice Targets:** Numerals, Time, Discourse, Structures, Articulation
**Level:** ★★★
**Group Size:** Pairs
**Repeat:** No
**Materials:** Student Workbook pages 26, 27, pencil
**Preparation:** None

**Background Information:** Partners have enrolled in a class entitled *Positive Roommate Communication, Time Organization, and Management*. This activity represents the homework for their class.

**Directions:** Pair students. Instruct partners to look at the Chore Chart and privately determine how often each chore needs to be done. Chores can be done daily, twice a week, weekly, bi-weekly, monthly, bi-monthly, every six months, yearly, etc. Instruct one partner to record his information on the first line under each chore and the other partner to use the second line.

To begin the activity one partner will choose a chore, record it on the workbook page, and inform his partner how often he thinks the chore should be performed. Partners will either agree or disagree. The discussion is a significant part of this activity. When a compromise is agreed upon, each partner will record it on the third line of the chart.

## REPLICA OF *CHORE CHART* FROM STUDENT WORKBOOK - PAGE 27

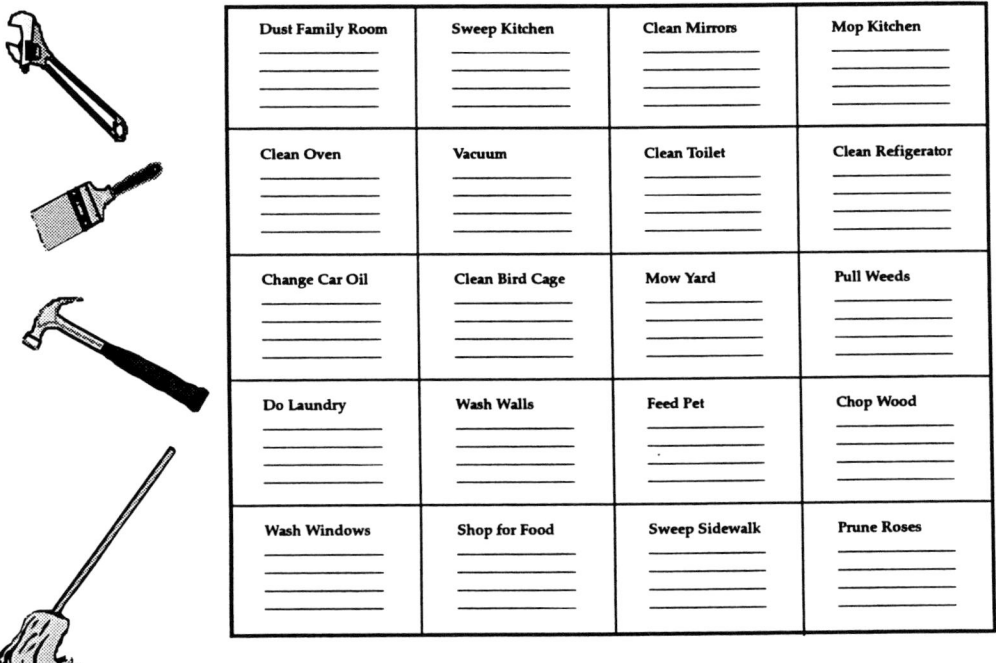

| Dust Family Room | Sweep Kitchen | Clean Mirrors | Mop Kitchen |
|---|---|---|---|
| Clean Oven | Vacuum | Clean Toilet | Clean Refrigerator |
| Change Car Oil | Clean Bird Cage | Mow Yard | Pull Weeds |
| Do Laundry | Wash Walls | Feed Pet | Chop Wood |
| Wash Windows | Shop for Food | Sweep Sidewalk | Prune Roses |

# BULL'S EYE

## GRETCHEN'S "TO DO" LIST

**Practice Targets:** Discourse, Structures, Articulation
**Level:** ★★★
**Group Size:** Pairs
**Repeat:** Yes, twice
**Materials:** Student Workbook pages 28, 29, 30, pencil
**Preparation:** None

**Background Information:** Gretchen has invited her family over for Sunday brunch. She has accomplished some of her tasks but she still has several things to do before the family arrives. Her friend, who has arrived to help with some of the chores, spots the list on the table and asks Gretchen what has already been done.

**Directions:** Pair students. Assign one partner to the role of Gretchen. Inform the other partner that he will become Gretchen's friend. Instruct partners to look at the *To Do* List on the Student Workbook page. Gretchen will:
1. privately decide several tasks which she has accomplished
2. when she did them
3. record that information on the Workbook page under her name.

Gretchen's friend will generate a list of questions related to the tasks.
Encourage him be creative with his questions and to focus on these areas:
- if Gretchen completed the chore
- if completed, when the task was done (yesterday, two days ago, this morning, etc.
- if the task was not done, when Gretchen plans to do it (a little later, much later, a specific time, tomorrow, a specific day, etc,)
- how long the task will take
- if Gretchen needs help with the task

Gretchen's friend will record her responses in the column labeled *Friend*.

# BULL'S EYE

**EXAMPLE:**

Sign the ASL equivalent of:
- **Friend:** "Have you done the grocery shopping yet?"
- **Gretchen:** "I bought food yesterday and it cost a fortune!"
- **Friend:** "Is your bathroom still a war zone?"
- **Gretchen:** "Yes."
- **Friend:** "When will you do that chore?"
- **Gretchen:** "I will do that this afternoon."
- **Friend:** "How long will it take?"
- **Gretchen:** "About 45 minutes. There is black mildew everywhere! Will you help me with that job? The rubber gloves look so good on you!"
- **Friend:** "Not a chance! But I will cut the flowers from the garden. Have you done that yet?"
- **Gretchen:** "I did that on Friday. They're in the bathroom serving as air freshener!"

•••••••••••••••••••••••••••••••••••••••••••••••••••••••••••••••••••••••••••••••••••••••••••••

## REPLICA OF *GRETCHEN'S "TO DO" LIST* FROM STUDENT WORKBOOK - PAGE 30

| Gretchen | Friend | Friend |
|---|---|---|
| \_\_\_\_\_ food | \_\_\_\_\_ food | \_\_\_\_\_ food |
| \_\_\_\_\_ bathroom | \_\_\_\_\_ bathroom | \_\_\_\_\_ bathroom |
| \_\_\_\_\_ flowers | \_\_\_\_\_ flowers | \_\_\_\_\_ flowers |
| \_\_\_\_\_ dog | \_\_\_\_\_ dog | \_\_\_\_\_ dog |
| \_\_\_\_\_ cookies | \_\_\_\_\_ cookies | \_\_\_\_\_ cookies |
| \_\_\_\_\_ bed | \_\_\_\_\_ bed | \_\_\_\_\_ bed |
| \_\_\_\_\_ windows | \_\_\_\_\_ windows | \_\_\_\_\_ windows |
| \_\_\_\_\_ vacuum | \_\_\_\_\_ vacuum | \_\_\_\_\_ vacuum |
| \_\_\_\_\_ floors | \_\_\_\_\_ floors | \_\_\_\_\_ floors |
| \_\_\_\_\_ table | \_\_\_\_\_ table | \_\_\_\_\_ table |
| \_\_\_\_\_ decorate | \_\_\_\_\_ decorate | \_\_\_\_\_ decorate |

# BULL'S EYE

## EMPLOYMENT AGENCY NETWORKING

**Practice Targets:** Time, Discourse, Structures, Articulation
**Level:** ★★★
**Group Size:** Pairs
**Repeat:** No
**Materials:** Student Workbook pages 31, 32, 33, pencil
**Preparation:** None

**Background Information:** Partners manage two different employment agencies, Acme and Mecca. Each partner has five clients. Each partner also has five job openings to fill. The job openings available in each agency do not exactly match the talents of the clients on their rosters. Partners have decided to combine their efforts to find more suitable positions for each of the clients described.

**Directions:** Pair students. Assign one partner the role of the manager of the Acme Employment Agency and the other partner the role of the manager of the Mecca Employment Agency. Instruct each partner to read the information provided on their specific Workbook page.

The manager for Acme will begin by describing one of his client's work experience and history. His partner will look over the job openings on his page and, if appropriate, suggest a client who may be able to fill the opening. Both partners will pencil in the name of the suggested person. Mecca's manager will continue the activity by describing one of his client's work experience and history while his partner searches for a suitable job opening. Partners will continue in this
manner until each of the ten clients have been discussed.

During the course of the discussion, it is possible that one client may be more suited to a particular job already suggested for someone else. Partners should continue to evaluate their decisions and make changes as needed. The goal of the partners is to fill as many positions with qualified candidates, however, it is possible that some clients will not be a "perfect match" for any job.

# BULL'S EYE

## EMPLOYMENT AGENCY NETWORKING

REPLICA OF *EMPLOYMENT AGENCY NETWORKING* FROM STUDENT WORKBOOK - PAGES 33, 34

### ACME EMPLOYMENT AGENCY

**A**

| Your Clients | Positions Open |
|---|---|
| **Name:** Miss Take<br>**Long Ago:** Economics Professor<br>**Recently:** Graduate Student<br>**Currently:** Unemployed  | Chef, specializing in fancy desserts<br>Candidates:_____ |
| **Name:** Miss Fortune<br>**Long Ago:** Dancer<br>**Recently:** Owned Dry Cleaners<br>**Currently:** House Cleaner  | Clerk In Bookstore<br>Candidates:_____ |
| **Name:** Albey C. Ingya<br>**Long Ago:** Sold Used Movies<br>**Recently:** Taught Adult Education<br>**Currently:** Film Producer  | Medical Consultant in the Brewers<br>Candidates:_____ |
| **Name:** Ken Wright<br>**Long Ago:** Dancer<br>**Recently:** Author of Dance Book<br>**Currently:** Dance Teacher | Bubble Gum Tester<br>Candidates:_____ |
| **Name:** Dusty Saw<br>**Long Ago:** Cabinet Maker<br>**Recently:** Chef<br>**Currently:** Builder | Manager of Studio for injured dancers<br>Candidates:_____ |

### MECCA EMPLOYMENT AGENCY

**B**

| Your Clients | Positions Open |
|---|---|
| **Name:** Can T. Wok<br>**Long Ago:** Student<br>**Recently:** Student<br>**Currently:** Food Taster  | Hurry Up Cleaners; Crew Manager<br>Candidates:_____ |
| **Name:** Mr. C. Lean<br>**Long Ago:** Chef<br>**Recently:** Butler<br>**Currently:** Athletic Trainer  | Cable Access Instructor<br>Candidates:_____ |
| **Name:** Ms. B. T. Krocker<br>**Long Ago:** Model<br>**Recently:** Baker<br>**Currently:** Professor of Home Economics  | T.V. Personality for "This Ugly House"<br>Candidates:_____ |
| **Name:** Mr. Will Sell<br>**Long Ago:** Sold Books<br>**Recently:** Sold Clothing<br>**Currently:** Sells Cars  | Financial Planner for the Bank of Rupt<br>Candidates:_____ |
| **Name:** Dr. Morey Paine<br>**Long Ago:** Dance trainer<br>**Recently:** Student<br>**Currently:** Doctor of Sports Medicine  | Spokesperson for "Auto-Dance" magazine<br>Candidates:_____ |

# BULL'S EYE

## OILS AND AROMAS

**Practice Targets:** Discourse, Structures, Articulation
**Level:** ★★★
**Group Size:** Pairs
**Repeat:** Yes
**Materials:** Student Workbook pages 35, 36, 37, pencil
**Preparation:** None

**Directions:** Pair students. Assign a Workbook page to each partner. Instruct partners to read the information on their page and develop a number of questions related to the oils, symptoms and applications. Partners can use the note pad to jot down concepts or drawings rather than complete English sentences. When partners are ready, instruct them to look at the same page in the Workbook. The partner who was assigned to that page will ask the questions he developed while his partner looks at the chart, finds the information and answers the question. Encourage partners to check for accurate answers. Partners will reverse roles.

**Example questions: (Students would sign the ASL equivalent:)**
Looking at the first page, a partner might ask:
1. How many different ways can I use anise seed?
2. How do I take anise seed?
3. What symptoms can anise seed relieve?

Students may want to generate questions like the following: (Sign the ASL equivalent)
1. I have varicose veins. What can help?
2. I need an expectorant. Any suggestions?
3. I have cut my finger. What would help?

Conversation continues in this manner until partners have each taken a turn.

# BULL'S EYE

## OILS AND AROMAS

REPLICA OF *OILS AND AROMAS* FROM STUDENT WORKBOOK - PAGES 36, 37

**A**

| OIL | GOOD FOR... | APPLICATION OPTIONS |
|---|---|---|
| ANISE SEED | hay fever, cramps, sinusitis, coughs | drops in water, tea, seasoning |
| BASIL | asthma, mental fatigue | drops in water, inhalation, massage oil |
| FENNEL | constipation, flatulence, hangover | bath, compress, drops in water, tea |
| CYPRESS | antiseptic, influenza, varicose veins | bath, inhalation, massage oil |
| CINNAMON | strengthens heart, toothache, pain reliever | tea, mouthwash |
| EUCALYPTUS | rheumatism, wounds, fevers, sore throat | drops, inhalation, massage oil, tea |
| JASMINE | stimulant, colds, obesity, expectorant | drops, massage oil, compress, tea |

**B**

| OIL | GOOD FOR... | APPLICATION OPTIONS |
|---|---|---|
| LAVENDER | burns, spider bites, energy balance, flatulence | bath, compress, inhalation |
| SANDLEWOOD | acne, dandruff, sore throat, nausea | facial compress, lotions, gargle, inhalation |
| PEPPERMINT | asthma, migraine head-aches, nervous disorders | bath, drops, inhalation, massage oil |
| CLARY SAGE | boils, PMS, depression | bath, deodorant, massage oil |
| CHAMOMILE | gingivitis, teething, wounds, menopause | lotion, tea, inhalation |
| BLACK PEPPER | colds, toothache, heart-burn, vertigo, burns fat | drops in water, tea, seasoning |
| GERANIUM | depression, ulcers, shingles, excema | bath drops, inhalation, massage oil |

# BULL'S EYE

## HEALING STONES

**Practice Targets:** Structures, Discourse, Articulation
**Level:** ★★★
**Group Size:** Pairs
**Repeat:** Yes
**Materials:** Student Workbook pages 39, 41, 42, pencil
**Preparation:** None

**Directions:** Pair students. Instruct partners to read the information on the Workbook page and develop several questions related to the stones and their specific healing properties. The Workbook page can simply provide a basis for a conversation about stones or students can use the sheet of paper to record notes or drawings that will help them remember the questions. When partners are ready, they will both look at the Workbook page. One student will begin by asking his partner the first question he developed. His partner will search the page and answer the question. If the answer is sufficient and correct, his partner will ask a question. Partners will continue to ask and answer questions until time is up.

**Example questions: (Students would sign the ASL equivalent:)**

1. What is the difference between what blue tourmaline does and what blue jade does?
2. Which stones will increase _____?
3. Two stones aid in communication. Which are they?
4. What will help my _____?

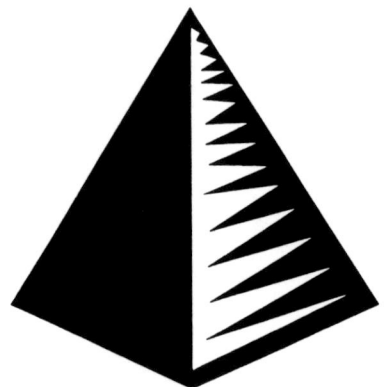

# BULL'S EYE

## *HEALING STONES*

REPLICA OF *HEALING STONES* FROM STUDENT WORKBOOK - PAGES 40, 41

**A**

| TOURMALINE | | CRYSTALS | |
|---|---|---|---|
| Yellow/Green | Communication | Blue/Green | Open-hearted acceptance |
| Pink/Green | Perseverance | Clear | Observation & clarity |
| Black | Healing house plants | Green | Assists in communication |
| Blue/Green | Open-hearted, giving | Light Green | Calming |
| Blue | Rejection of unwanted | Light Blue | Power |
| Yellow/Brown | Intellectual processing | Blue Tinge | Curbs impatience |
| Turquoise | Connectedness | Orange | Promotes happiness |
| Green/Dark. Green | Communicative abilities | Pink | Simplicity |
| | | Yellow | Energizing |
| | | Red | Dynamism |

**B**

| JADE | | ZIRCON | |
|---|---|---|---|
| Black | Balances | Brown | For headaches |
| Blue | Neutralizes | Green | Gregariousness |
| Brown/Grey | Relaxes | Pink | Spiritual growth |
| Green | Tranquility | Purple | Monetary resourcefulness |
| Lavender | Optimism | Red | Helps ear infections |
| Orange | Protection for gullible | White | Aura cleansing |
| White | Objectivity | | |
| Yellow | Understanding | | |

# BULL'S EYE

## MOTHER'S NATURE REMEDIES

**Practice Targets:** Structures, Discourse, Numerals, Time, Articulation
**Level:** ★★★
**Group Size:** Pairs
**Repeat:** Yes
**Materials:** Student Workbook pages 43, 44, 45, pencil

**Background Information:** The Community's Eye is a weekly publication for the Deaf community. Their reporter is interviewing the owner of the store Mother's Nature Remedies, which specializes in herbs and homeopathic cures.

**Directions:** Pair students. Assign one partner the role of the reporter. Instruct the reporter to use one page of the Student Workbook. Instruct the other student to take on the role of the store owner. He will work from the corresponding page in the Student Workbook.

Instruct the reporter to look at the ailments on his page. He should describe one of the ailments to the store owner. Instruct the store owner to choose one of the remedies from his side of the page and describe the natural treatment to the reporter. The reporter will record that information on the line of the Workbook page under the ailment with drawings or brief notes.

When the reporter has acquired all the needed information, instruct the students to switch roles. Each partner will continue to work from their same page. When the reporter becomes the owner, he will simply describe the naturopathic remedies from the other side of his page.

## MOTHER'S NATURE REMEDIES (the answers)

| | | | |
|---|---|---|---|
| Hiccoughs | Mix 3 oz. Rose petals, 2 oz. mint leaves, 1/2 oz. powdered cloves in bag under pillow | Heartburn | Chew 2 Tbsp. Uncooked oats |
| Ink on fingers | Rub fingers with unburned match | Sprayed by skunk | Bathe in tomato juice |
| Memory problems before exams | Eat sunflower & sesame seeds | Sunburned | Grate raw potato, rest peelings on area for 10 mn. |
| Swollen ankles | Soak for 20 min. daily in sea water | Bags under eyes | Pat area with wet tea bag |
| Stung by jellyfish | Apply vodka to area | Hungry during diet | Squeeze earlobe |
| Warts | Slice garlic, tape to area. Change 3 times daily for a week | Varicose veins | Soak cheese cloth in apple cider vinegar, wrap, elevate 2x daily for 30 min. |
| Athlete's foot | Grate 1 potato and wrap in clean cloth, apply to area | Ticks | Paint them with clear finger nail polish |

# BULL'S EYE

## MOTHER'S NATURE REMEDIES

**REPLICA OF** *MOTHER'S NATURES REMEDIES* **FROM STUDENT WORKBOOK - PAGES 44, 45**

**A**

| REPORTER QUESTIONS | STORE OWNER "CURES" |
|---|---|
| Hiccoughs | Paint it with clear fingernail polish |
| Ink on fingers | Bathe in tomato juice |
| Memory problems before exams | Pat area with wet tea bag |
| Swollen ankles | Chew 2 tbsp. uncooked oat flakes |
| Stung by jellyfish | Soak cheesecloth in apple cider vinegar, wrap, elevate twice daily for 30 min. |
| Warts | Squeeze earlobe |
| Athletes foot | Grate raw potato and rest peelings on area for 10 min. |

**B**

| REPORTER QUESTIONS | STORE OWNER "CURES" |
|---|---|
| Heartburn | Eat sunflower and sesame seeds |
| Sprayed by skunk | Apply vodka to area |
| Sunburned | Grate 1 potato, wrap in clean cloth, apply to area |
| Bags under eyes | Slice garlic, tape to area, change 3 times daily for a week |
| Hungry during diet | Rub fingers with unburned match |
| Varicose veins | Soak for 20 min. daily in sea water |
| Ticks | Mix 3 oz. Rose petals, 2 oz. Mint leaves, 1/2 oz. Powdered cloves, put in bag under pillow |

# BULL'S EYE

## CURE IT NATURALLY

**Practice Targets:** Numerals, Discourse, Structures, Time, Articulation
**Level:** ★★★
**Group Size:** Large
**Repeat:** Yes
**Materials:** *Ailment and Cure Cards*, separated
**Preparation:** Copy the *Ailment and Cure Cards* pages, cut out the cards. (Optional: laminate cards) Arrange an area in which students can mingle.

**Directions:** Distribute a *Cure Card* to one half of the students. Distribute an *Ailment Card* to the remaining students. Explain that the object of this activity is to find the correct cure for each ailment.

Instruct students to formulate an ASL statement about their *Ailment* or *Cure*. When ready, students can mingle in the open area of the room. When two students feel as though their *Ailment* and *Cure* match up, they can move to the side of the room. It is likely that some *Cures* and *Ailments* will be left mingling without a logical match. When this happens, encourage those students to questions pairs already matched. If a new match develops, the student without a match begins a new search.

When everyone has decided on a match, convene as a large group and discuss the combinations.

**EXAMPLE: (Students will sign the ASL equivalent:)**

| | |
|---|---|
| *Ailment* Student: | "I have garlic breath." |
| *Cure* Student 1: | "Blow your nose three times, keeping your eyelids pried open." |
| | |
| *Ailment* Student: | "I have garlic breath." |
| *Cure* Student 2: | "Soak bandage in witch hazel, place on affected area." |
| | |
| *Ailment* Student: | "I have garlic breath." |
| *Cure* Student 3: | "Place sliced cucumbers on affected area." |

**Note:** Each *Ailment* card corresponds with the correct *Cure* card in the Teacher's Manual.

# BULL'S EYE

## *HYPOCHONDRIAC*

**Practice Targets:** Structures, Descriptors, Numerals, Discourse, Time, Articulation
**Level:** ★★★
**Group Size:** Large or small
**Repeat:** Yes
**Materials:** *Ailment and Cure Cards*, separated
**Preparation:** Copy the *Ailment and Cure Cards* pages, cut out the cards. (Optional: laminate cards) Arrange an area in which students can mingle.

**Directions:** Students will invent wild and outrageous stories about how they came down with the ailment on the card. Distribute an *Ailment Card* to each student. Instruct students to invent a short scenario describing how they came down with their dreaded ailment or how they found out about it. When students are ready, give each a few minutes to describe their medical woes to the class.

## *MIRACLE CURES!*

**Practice Targets:** Structures, Descriptors, Numerals, Discourse, Time, Articulation
**Level:** ★★★
**Group Size:** Large or small
**Repeat:** Yes
**Materials:** *Ailment and Cure Cards*, separated
**Preparation:** Copy the *Ailment and Cure Cards* pages, cut out the cards. (Optional: laminate cards) Arrange an area in which students can mingle.

**Directions:** Students will invent a dreaded ailment that they have cured with the directions on their *Cure Card*.

Distribute a *Cure Card* to each student. Give students time to develop a short scenario in which they will describe their ailment and their long and arduous search for a cure. Instruct students to include at least two other cures they tried which were unsuccessful.

When students are ready, each will be given a few minutes to describe their homeopathic break through to the class.

# BULL'S EYE

## AILMENT AND CURE CARDS *(the answers)*

| AILMENTS | CURES |
|---|---|
| **Cold Sores** | Cut clove of garlic, rub on affected area |
| **Brittle Fingernails** | Drink 1/2 cup parsnip juice once a day |
| **Dark Circles Under Eyes** | Cut a fig in half, put each half on affected areas, rinse when done |
| **Stomach Ache** | Mix 2 Tbsp. Baking soda with cup of water, drink |

# BULL'S EYE

## AILMENT AND CURE CARDS *(the answers)*

| AILMENTS | CURES |
|---|---|
| Rheumatism | Make fire using elmwood, sit near it |
| Body Odor | Grate turnip, squeeze juice through cheese cloth to get 2 tsp., Rub area with juice |
| Garlic Breath | Eat slice of lemon with salt on it |
| Have a Cold | Heat 1 Tbsp. Fresh lemon rind with equal amount of water, dab of butter and honey. Drink. |

# BULL'S EYE

## AILMENT AND CURE CARDS  (the answers)

| AILMENTS | CURES |
|---|---|
| Stuffy Nose | To 1 pt. Of distilled water, add 1 tsp. Salt. Add cologne for scent and sniff |
| Something in Eye | Blow nose 3 times, keeping eyelids pried open |
| Tired Eyes | Place sliced cucumbers on affected area |
| Black Eye | Soak bandage in witch hazel, place on affected area, raise feet |

# BULL'S EYE

## AILMENT AND CURE CARDS *(the answers)*

| AILMENTS | CURES |
|---|---|
| Fleas in House | Spread camomile flowers around home |
| Face Wrinkles | Mix 1 egg yolk, 1/2 tsp. Lemon juice, 1/2 tsp. Olive oil, spread on area, wait, wash |
| Sore Throat | Chew on licorice root |
| Constipated | Mix equal parts of molasses and honey, drink |

# BULL'S EYE

## AILMENT AND CURE CARDS *(the answers)*

| AILMENTS | CURES |
|---|---|
| Burns | Soak linen cloth in linseed oil, wrap affected area |
| Calluses on Feet | Walk barefoot on sand |
| Fever | Mix 1 1/2 tsp cream of tartar, 1/2 tsp. Lemon juice, 1/2 tsp honey to make 1 pt. Drink. |
| Gout | Eat bowlful of cherries first day, then 8 cherries daily thereafter |

# BULL'S EYE

## AILMENT AND CURE CARDS *(the answers)*

**AILMENTS**

**CURES**

| | |
|---|---|
| Dull Hair | Rinse with chamomile tea after washing |
| Terrible Nightmares | Sprinkle essence of anise on pillow |
| Walk in Sleep | Place piece of wet carpet by bedside |

# BULL'S EYE

## HOW MUCH, HOW MANY SURVEY

**Practice Targets:** Numerals, Time, Discourse, Structures, Articulation
**Level:** ★★★
**Group Size:** Large or small
**Repeat:** No
**Materials:** Student Workbook pages 46, 47, pencil
**Preparation:** None

**Directions:** Assign students to a group, large or small. Either work with the group and develop one ASL question for each of the phrases or instruct students to develop their own ASL questions. The students will ask the same questions to eight other classmates and record their answers on the Workbook page.

Allow time for students to complete the survey and reconvene as a group to discuss the results.

**Note: As an extension of this activity, consider creating a graph of the responses of the students.**

REPLICA OF *HOW MUCH, HOW MANY SURVEY* FROM STUDENT WORKBOOK - PAGE 47

| | | | | | | |
|---|---|---|---|---|---|---|
| 1. Spent the most money yesterday | | | | | | |
| 2. Took the longest vacation last year | | | | | | |
| 3. Watched the most T.V. last night | | | | | | |
| 4. Ate the largest breakfast this morning | | | | | | |
| 5. Saw the most movies in the last two weeks | | | | | | |
| 6. Has the largest family | | | | | | |
| 7. Has the oldest living relative | | | | | | |
| 8. Studied the most number of hours last night | | | | | | |
| 9. Exercises the most number of hours per week | | | | | | |
| 10. Traveled the farthest to school | | | | | | |
| 11. Has the most number of pets | | | | | | |

# BULL'S EYE

## OUT TO LUNCH

**Practice Targets:** Structures, Discourse, Numerals, Articulation, Time
**Group Size:** Pairs
**Repeat:** No
**Materials:** Student Workbook pages 49, 50, 51, pencil
**Preparation:** None

**Background Information:** Partners are students from the Hampton Culinary Arts Institute. They have decided to go out for lunch and are in the process of finalizing their restaurant choice. This is a difficult task since both of them tend to be methodical and slow to make any decision!

**Directions:** Pair students. Assign a separate Workbook page to each partner. Instruct partners to read the restaurant ads and then use the phrases on their pages to develop ASL questions. (The phrases on one partners relate to the ads on the other partner's page.)

Instruct one partner to begin by forming an ASL question for his partner. His partner will look at the ads on his page and answer the question in ASL. The first partner will record the answer in note for, or by drawing. Do not use complete English sentences.

Partners take turns gathering information about each of the restaurants until all of the questions have been answered.

# BULL'S EYE

## OUT TO LUNCH

REPLICAS OF *OUT TO LUNCH* FROM STUDENT WORKBOOK - PAGES 50, 51

**A**

1. mussels?_____
2. chef's name_____
3. listed cost for lunch?_____ dinner?_____
4. locations?_____
5. reservations needed?_____
6. meatloaf?_____
7. slogans?_____
8. hours?_____
9. phone number?_____
10. interesting menu items_____
11. wine served?_____
12. kind of wine?_____
13. eat outside?_____
14. your choice of restaurant?_____

---

**WINGS PLACE**
dine in or take out
excellent Mandarin cuisine
rice and tea with each meal
vegetarian orders welcome

Emperor Chicken
Spicy beef or chicken
Pot Stickers!

150 menu items

---

**Harold's Haute Cuisine**
*"on the Promenade"*

Live Jazz Nightly

our specialties include:
blackened river trout
fresh mussels with wine sauce
shrimp tomato fettucine
veal with orange sauce
and of course our famous dessert tray!

**RESERVATIONS: 560 - 4459**

---

**B**

**OLDE TOWNE BUFFET**
*"your mom would approve"*

featuring:
- Salisbury Steak with Mushroom Gravy
- Chicken and Dumplings
- Aunt Millie's Meat Loaf
- Fried codfish
- Potatoes O'Brien
- Boiled Mixed Vegetables
- Tuna Casserole baked with Chips

**Lunch $4.89   Dinner $6.29**

Open Everyday 8 -8

---

**ANTONIO'S**
*The KING of Pasta!*

Lunch and Dinner served daily
Enjoy a glass of Chianti
in our new courtyard!

featuring fresh pasta
Spaghetti, Lasagna, Pizza....

**THE BEST IN TOWN!**
220 Church St.
566-4655

*All meals lovingly
prepared by Antonio himself!*

---

1. hours listed?_____
2. serves fish?_____
3. music?_____
4. mussels?_____
5. spicy food?_____
6. vegetarian food?_____
7. specialties_____
8. most menu items?_____ How many?_____
9. delicious desserts?_____
10. reservations needed?_____
11. slogans_____
12. phone numbers?_____
13. take out food?_____
14. your choice of restaurant?_____

# BULL'S EYE

## PERSONAL TIME LINES

**Practice Targets:** Time, Discourse, Structures, Articulation
**Group Size:** Pairs
**Repeat:** Yes (limited)
**Materials:** Student Workbook pages 52, 53, pencil
**Preparation:** None

**Background Information:** Students are involved in a class called Personal Genealogy. The first assignment for each student is to create a timeline of his life, indicating the important events by year.

**Directions:** Pair students. Instruct students to look at the Workbook page and consider five important events that have occurred in their lives. Below the timeline students will record the year. Above each year students will draw a picture which represents the event.

When partners are ready one can be describing his timeline. Instruct the other partner to use a blank timeline and record the events his partner describes. (Partners are instructed not to look at each other's timeline until the descriptions are complete.)

Partners each take a turn describing the events in their lives and recording the events of their partner's life. When partners have completed the task, they can compare drawings and discuss discrepancies. When partners are satisfied with the completed work, they can move on to a new partner and repeat the description part of the activity.

### PERSONAL TIME LINE EXAMPLE

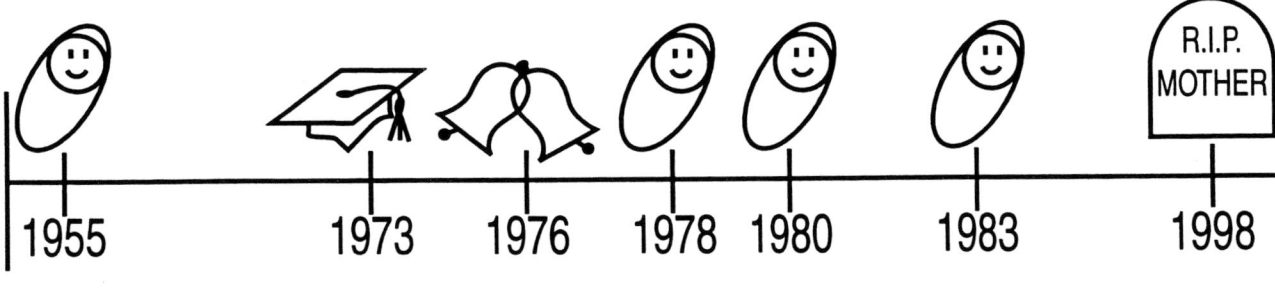

1955 Born    1973 H.S. graduation    1978 daughter    1980 daughter
             1976 Married                              1983 son

**Note:** Use this activity for the practice of ASL conjunctions such as: "wrong," "frustrate," "hit," "find," "happen."

# BULL'S EYE

## THE WEEKEND

**Practice Targets:** Structures, Numerals, Discourse, Articulation
**Group Size:** Small
**Repeat:** No
**Materials:** Student Workbook pages 54, 55, pencil
**Preparation:** None

**Background Information:** A group of friends is planning a get-away to a mountain cabin.

**Directions:** Assign students to a small group. Instruct students to look over the Student Workbook page. Using the workbook page as a guide students will plan their weekend. Groups should discuss who will drive, where they will meet, what games they will play, the meals that will be served, who will be responsible for cooking and cleaning, etc. Together they will create a plan for their weekend activities.

When the group has reached a consensus, each person will fill in the Student Workbook page.

Each group can make a short presentation describing their weekend.

### REPLICA OF *THE WEEKEND* FROM STUDENT WORKBOOK - PAGE 55

DRIVER:_____ CAR SEATS:_____ DESTINATION:_____
MEETING PLACE:_____ DAY AND TIME:_____

| FRI. NIGHT MEAL | SAT. DINNER MEAL | GAMES |
|---|---|---|
| what?_____ | what?_____ | 1._____ |
| chef:_____ | chef:_____ | 2._____ |
| clean up:_____ | clean up:_____ | 3._____ |

| SAT. A.M. MEAL | SUN A.M. MEAL | FINAL CLEAN-UP |
|---|---|---|
| what?_____ | what?_____ | kitchen:_____ |
| chef:_____ | chef:_____ | beds:_____ |
| clean up:_____ | clean up:_____ | living room:_____ |

| SAT. NOON MEAL | SUN. NOON MEAL | ITINERARY |
|---|---|---|
| what?_____ | what?_____ | 1._____ |
| chef:_____ | chef:_____ | 2._____ |
| clean up:_____ | clean up:_____ | 3._____ |
| | | 4._____ |
| | | 5._____ |

# BULL'S EYE

## WACKO WEDDINGS

**Practice Targets:** Descriptives, Structures, Discourse, Articulation
**Level:** ★★★★
**Group Size:** Small
**Repeat:** No
**Materials:** Student Workbook pages 56, 57, pencil
**Preparation:** None

**Background Information:** Students are part of the wildly popular wedding service, *Wacko Weddings*, whose reputation for planning unusual an unique weddings is unsurpassed. *Wacko Weddings* designed and implemented the wedding of the couple who jumped off a San Francisco bridge in matching bungi cords just as they said, "I do." They were also responsible for the underwater wedding on killer whales in Baja, California.

**Directions:** Assign students to a small group. Instruct them to use the Workbook page as a guide in planning a unique and unusual wedding. Explain that the clients have left the creativity up to the staff and that money is no object. Caution them that the wedding plans must be reasonably safe and definitely legal.

Once student groups have developed a plan each member will use the Student Workbook page to record a drawing of their final plan.

Inform each group that they will also be responsible for planning a three to five minute presentation for the bride and groom in an attempt to promote their plan over the other plans within the firm. Encourage groups to add creativity to their presentations such as costumes, props, etc.

## REPLICA OF *WACKO WEDDINGS* FROM STUDENT WORKBOOK - PAGE 57

Date:_____   Time:_____

| Theme | Location | Special Effects | Bridal Costumes |
|---|---|---|---|
| | | | |
| **Groom Costume** | **Bridesmaids & Groomsmen** | **Entertainment** | **Food & Beverages** |
| | | | |

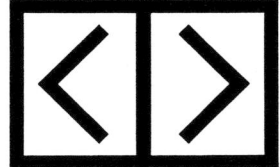

# TARGET RANGE

## 30 - 50 Minute Activities

Games in this section are divided into units. Each unit contains several activities of varying difficulty. These units are designed to be played over the course of a student's ASL development. Begin with the easy activities in the early part of the year. As the skills of the students improve, return to more challenging games in the unit. I found that each time we returned to the unit, the students' increased familiarity with the unit and its characters generated an increase in comfort. That comfort generated more risk-taking and more learning.

Many of the activities in this section focus on role play which has a great deal of flexibility as well as a rather unique and unpredictable nature. The addition of props and costumes increases student participation as well as their enjoyment!

# TARGET RANGE

## *THE McGREEVY FAMILY TREE*

The activities in *The Mcgreevy Family Tree* begin the focus of Target Range with activities that involve some structure and some role play. The unit focuses specifically on family signs and relationships. For the role play activities students can develop personalities based on the pictures. Encourage students to develop characters with some depth and to maintain their character attributes during the role play. Sometimes a bit of costume or a hint of idiosyscrancy will aid in the development of a character.

# TARGET RANGE

## THE McGREEVY FAMILY TREE

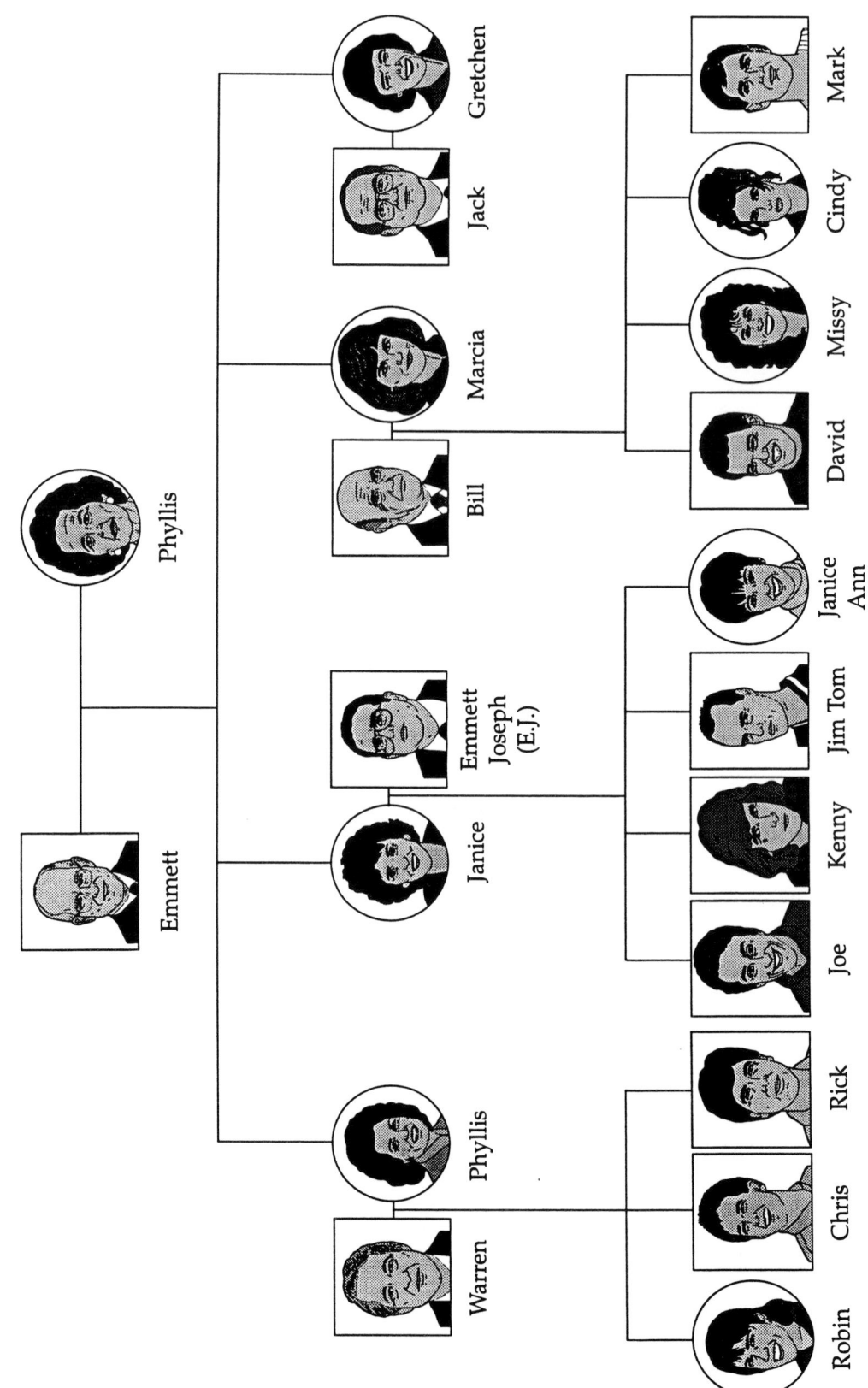

# TARGET RANGE

## *THE McGREEVY FAMILY TREE*

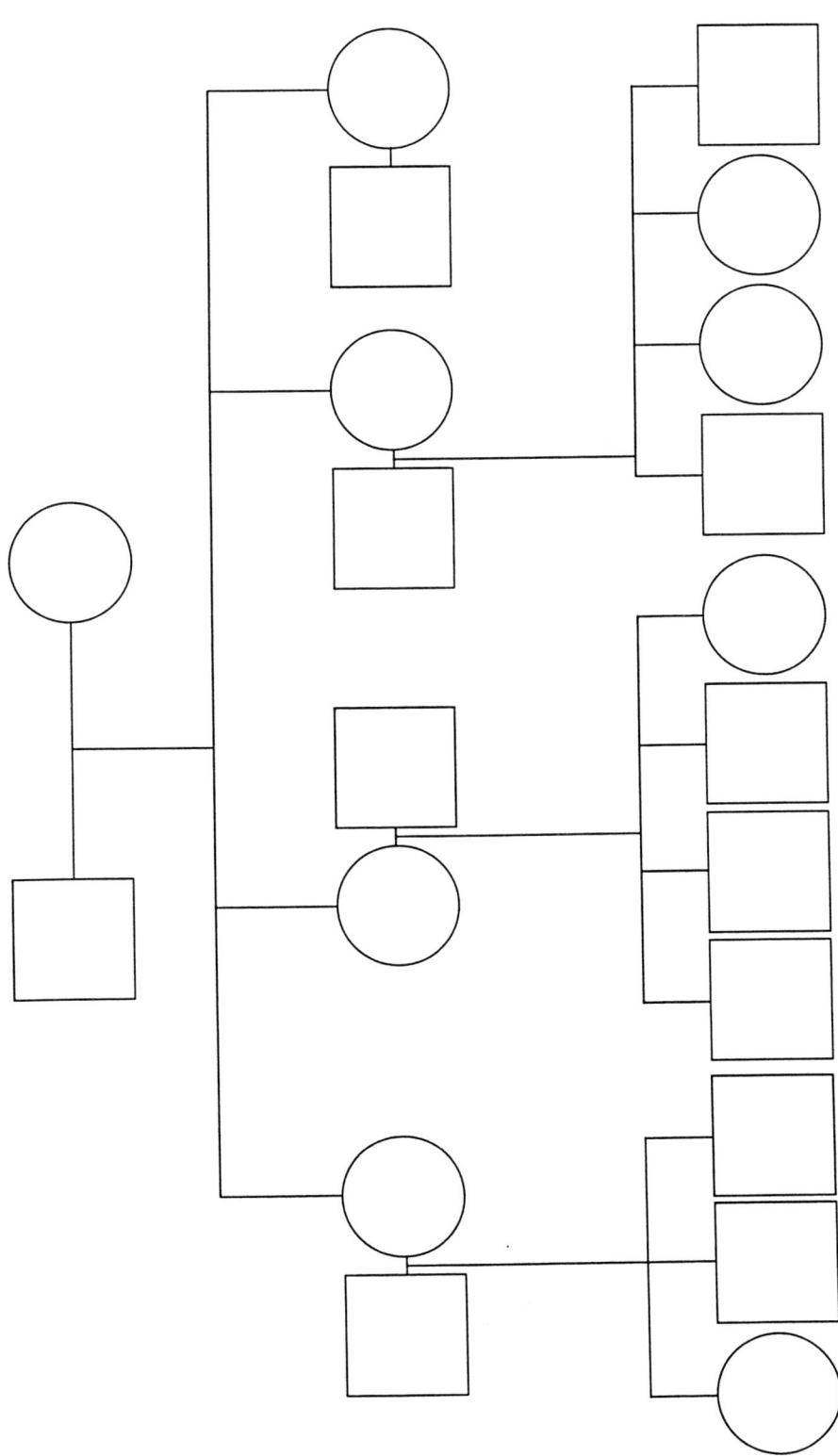

 **TARGET RANGE**

## *THE McGREEVY FAMILY TREE*
**Activity 1: Meet the McGreevy Family**

**Practice Targets:** Numerals, Discourse, Descriptors, Structures
**Level:** ★★
**Group Size:** Large
**Repeat:** Yes
**Materials:** Student Workbook page 61, pencil
**Preparation:** Make a transparency of the blank *Meet the McGreevy Family* page 87 in the Teacher's Manual.

**Directions:** Instruct students to turn to the Workbook page entitled *Meet the McGreevy Family*. Use the answers in the Teacher's Manual to introduce the McGreevy Family. Describe family members, their names and their relationships within the family. Students will record that information in the appropriate circles and squares on the Workbook page.

# TARGET RANGE

## THE McGREEVY FAMILY TREE
### Activity 2: Personal Family Trees

**Practice Targets:** Discourse, Descriptors, Structures, Articulation
**Level:** ★★
**Group Size:** Pairs
**Repeat:** Yes, Three times
**Materials:** Student Workbook pages 62, 63, pencil
**Preparation:** None

**Directions:** Pair students. Instruct each student to draw a real or imaginary family tree in the top left quadrant of the Workbook page. The family tree should include at least three generations. Partner A will begin by describing his family tree. Partner B will draw what he understands and then describe the family tree. Partner A will check for accuracy by asking for clarification, not by looking at the drawing. When partners are satisfied, they can look at the drawing together. Partners will reverse roles.

**Note:** This activity can be done a total of three times. Draw the first Family Tree in the upper left quadrant of the page. Use the other three quadrants when partners change.

### REPLICA OF *PERSONAL FAMILY TREES* FROM STUDENT WORKBOOK - PAGE 63

# TARGET RANGE

## THE McGREEVY FAMILY TREE
### Activity 3: Family Business

**Practice Targets:** Discourse, Structures, Articulation
**Level:** ★★
**Group Size:** Pairs
**Repeat:** No
**Materials:** Student Workbook pages 64, 65, pencil
**Preparation:** None

**Directions:** Pair students. Instruct partners to turn to the corresponding Student Workbook page. Assign each partner one side of the page, A or B.

Using their own or fabricated family information, instruct partners to privately fill in the blanks for family members' ages and occupations. Partner A will begin by signing his information. Partner B will record it on the Workbook page. Partners are not to share their written information until the end of the activity. Encourage students to focus on the use of clarification strategies as they check for accuracy.

When partners are satisfied, partners will reverse roles. Students can share their written work at the end of the activity.

### REPLICA OF *FAMILY BUSINESS* FROM STUDENT WORKBOOK - PAGE 65

| A<br>Relationship | Age | Occupation | B<br>Relationship | Age | Occupation |
|---|---|---|---|---|---|
| 1. Grandfather | ____ | _____ | 1. Grandfather | ____ | _____ |
| 2. Grandmother | ____ | _____ | 2. Grandmother | ____ | _____ |
| 3. Aunt | ____ | _____ | 3. Aunt | ____ | _____ |
| 4. Uncle | ____ | _____ | 4. Uncle | ____ | _____ |
| 5. Cousin | ____ | _____ | 5. Cousin | ____ | _____ |
| 6. Brother | ____ | _____ | 6. Brother | ____ | _____ |
| 7. Sister | ____ | _____ | 7. Sister | ____ | _____ |
| 8. Niece | ____ | _____ | 8. Niece | ____ | _____ |
| 9. Nephew | ____ | _____ | 9. Nephew | ____ | _____ |
| 10._____ | ____ | _____ | 10._____ | ____ | _____ |
| 11._____ | ____ | _____ | 11._____ | ____ | _____ |

# TARGET RANGE

## *THE McGREEVY FAMILY TREE*
### Activity 4: McGreevy Family Relationships

**Practice Targets:** Structures, Discourse, Articulation
**Level:** ★★★
**Group Size:** Large
**Repeat:** Yes
**Materials:** *Family Relationship Cards* (at least one for each student)
**Preparation:** Copy the *Family Relationship Cards* and cut them out. Make enough of the cards so that each student has at least one card. There are 21 family members. Optional: laminate the cards. Create a blank transparency of the *Meet the McGreevy Family*. Create a second transparency with the correct names and positions filled in.

**Directions:** The object of this activity is to figure out the identity of the family member on the card and their position in the family.

Distribute a *Family Relationship Card* to each student. Instruct students to introduce themselves and ask each other questions in an attempt to discover their own identities. Encourage them to share the information clues they have and help each other. Students may find it helpful to physically arrange themselves similar to the displayed family tree.

When families are united, each of them can introduce themselves and describe their position in the family tree.

**Notes:**
1. For smaller groups, play the game without the cousin cards.
2. Offer some students more than one card.
3. Three cards (Ricky, Missy, Joe) are more ambiguous and therefore more challenging to figure out. Students who have these cards will need to rely on other information.

## ANSWERS TO THE FAMILY RELATIONSHIPS

| | | |
|---|---|---|
| wife of Emmett (Phyllis) mother-in-law of Janice | sister of Mark (Missy) daughter of Marcia | brother-in-law of Warren (Bill) father of Mark |
| husband of Phyllis (Warren) (Gretchen) father of Chris | grandson of Emmett (Mark) cousin of Rick, Kenny | sister-in-law of Warren and Bill aunt of Kenny |
| aunt of Chris and Missy (Janice) mother of Janice Ann | nephew of Bill, Jack, Warren (Kenny) Brother of Joe and Jim Tom | cousin of Joe (Chris) brother of Rick |
| parent of Missy (Marcia) daughter of Emmett | niece of Phyllis, Bill, Jack (Janice Ann) cousin of Rick and Mark | nephew of Jack, Bill, Janice (Rick) grandson of Emmett |
| son-in-law of Phyllis (Jack) (Cindy) brother-in-law of Warren, Bill | father of Phyllis (Emmett) husband of Phyllis | niece of Gretchen, E.J., Phyllis sister of Missy |
| niece of Bill (Robin) daughter of Phyllis | daughter of Phyllis (Phyllis) sister of Marcia, E.J., Gretchen | grandson of Phyllis (Joe) cousin of Robin and Missy |
| cousin to Chris and Joe (David) brother of Mark | uncle of Robin and Cindy (E.J.) brother-in-law of Warren, Bill, Jack | son of E.J. (Jim Tom) brother of Joe and Kenny |

# TARGET RANGE

## THE McGREEVY FAMILY TREE

**FAMILY RELATIONSHIP CARDS**

| | |
|---|---|
| wife of Emmett<br>mother-in-law of Janice | father of Phyllis<br>husband of Phyllis |
| husband of Phyllis<br>father of Chris | daughter of Phyllis<br>sister of Marcia, E.J., Gretchen |
| aunt of Chris and Missy<br>mother of Janice Ann | uncle of Robin and Cindy<br>brother-in-law of Warren, Bill, Jack |
| parent of Missy<br>daughter of Emmett | brother-in-law of Warren<br>father of Mark |
| son-in-law of Phyllis<br>brother-in-law of Warren, Bill | sister-in-law of Warren and Bill<br>aunt of Kenny |
| niece of Bill<br>daughter of Phyllis | cousin of Joe<br>brother of Rick |

# TARGET RANGE

## THE McGREEVY FAMILY TREE

FAMILY RELATIONSHIP CARDS CONT.

| | |
|---|---|
| cousin to Chris and Joe<br>brother of Mark | nephew of Jack, Bill, Janice<br>grandson of Emmett |
| sister of Mark<br>daughter of Marcia | niece of Gretchen, E.J., Phyllis<br>sister of Missy |
| grandson of Emmett<br>cousin of Rick, Kenny | grandson of Phyllis<br>cousin of Robin and Missy |
| nephew of Bill, Jack, Warren<br>Brother of Joe and Jim Tom | son of E.J.<br>brother of Joe and Kenny |
| niece of Phyllis, Bill, Jack<br>cousin of Rick and Mark | |

# TARGET RANGE

## THE McGREEVY FAMILY TREE
### Activity 5: McGreevy Family Reunion

**Practice Targets:** Structures, Descriptors, Discourse, Articulation
**Level:** ★★★★
**Group Size:** Large
**Repeat:** Yes
**Materials:** Names of McGreevy Family Members
**Preparation:** Optional: bring props, jewelry, scarves, hats, etc. to add to the realism of the reunion. You may also want to give awards for the "McGreevy family's most unusual 20 years," "the McGreevy family's most exciting 20 years," etc.

**Background:** The McGreevy family is planning their first family reunion in 20 years. Since the family members live in 12 different states, they have a lot of catching up to do. Family members have been asked to make a short presentation (3 - 5 minutes) about what's been happening in their lives.

**Directions:** Assign a family member's name to each student. Explain that each family will be responsible for developing a 3 - 5 minute presentation which should include references to 20 years ago, 10 years ago, 5 years ago, their present and their future. Encourage students to add anecdotes or family stories and bring costumes which will enhance their presentations.

Instruct students to find their family members and meet to develop their family history. Students who draw the cousin cards should know that the youngest cousin, Mark, is now 19. Other cousins can determine their ages based on Mark's age. Allow a sufficient time for students to meet, plan and practice their presentations.

Arrange a time for presentations.

# TARGET RANGE

## ASK THE EXPERTS

The activities in *Ask the Experts* involve creating characters and role play as they relate to Deaf culture and the education of deaf children. Many of these activities are open-ended. Mirroring real life, partners or groups will determine the course of the conversation.

The unit focuses on the kinds of people many of us encounter in our journeys into the "field of deafness." Central to this unit are the biographies and business cards of the characters. Students will be able to use the information in the biographies to create, from the inside out, a persona for each of the activities. Using those characters, students will have numerous opportunities to discover some of the issues facing Deaf community today. Under the guise of role play students will be able to see some of those issues from different perspectives.

For these activities to be of most benefit it is important that students create characters with some depth and maintain those character attributes during the role play. Encourage students to take some time to consider what kind of life that character has, his/her attitudes, philosophies, mannerisms, and views on the world. Sometimes a bit of a costume or a hint of an idiosyncrasy will aid in the development of a character.

## BIOGRAPHIES

**Johnathon Fowler, Writer-Producer**

Johnathon was the only child of Deaf parents. He attended the California residential school for the Deaf, graduated and entered NTID. He currently serves on the NTID Alumni Board and volunteers one afternoon a week as a Boy Scout leader at the residential school. Johnathon is trying to get a career off the ground. He has written a few pieces for public television and has a made-for-TV movie in progress with an all Deaf cast. Johnathon is a firm believer in a residential school education for all Deaf children which includes the exclusive use of ASL in the classroom.

---

| 1778 NW 15th Ave | 823-9000 Voice |
| Burbank, CA 98777 | 823-8000 TDD |

**JOHNATHON FOWLER**

Writer-Producer

Television Programs for Deaf & Hearing Viewers

# TARGET RANGE

## ASK THE EXPERTS

### BIOGRAPHIES

**Dolly Sutton, Therapist**

Dolly Sutton, age 70, is still a spark plug. She is a respected therapist in the area. Growing up on a large farm full of corn fields in Indiana, Dolly's childhood could be described as wholesome and innocent. Dolly was an extremely bright little girl but she always appeared to be an observer. She also had a habit of responding to people only when she wanted to. Dolly attended a small one-room school house. During her school years she felt like an outcast. Her teacher described her as a dreamer. It wasn't until she was in high school that a visiting nurse discovered that Dolly was hard of hearing. For a while Dolly felt like even more of an outcast. It was in college that she decided to work for the betterment of other hard of hearing people. As president of the local chapter of Self Help for the Hard of Hearing Dolly meets many people who are in need of some therapy in order to deal with problems related to their hearing losses.

> **Dolly Sutton, BA, MSW, PhD**
> Therapist
>
> 578 Getoverit Street / Assist, ID 57899
> (365) 186-4398 (V/TTY)
>
> President of the Assist Chapter of SHHH

**John (Shorty) Muller, Small Business Owner**

John Muller (Shorty) grew up in Brooklyn. He is the father of a hearing impaired four year old daughter. Shorty and his wife suspected Ellen's deafness when she was about six months old but their pediatrician just told them that Ellen was a little "delayed" and that they should just give her time. The diagnosis of bilateral profound deafness was finally made when Ellen was almost two years old. Both Shorty and his wife are learning ASL. They are concerned by the fact that they feel ostracized and unwelcome by many members of the Deaf community.

> **Shorty's Sports Emporium**
>
> 4590 Scratchit Street
> Tie, AL 69488
> (405) 809-5000 (V/TDD)
>
> *specializing in adaptive sports equipment*

96

# TARGET RANGE

## ASK THE EXPERTS

### BIOGRAPHIES

**Marianne Rolling, Teacher of the Deaf**

Marianne Rolling grew up with many hard of hearing people in her family. Three Grandmothers, her father and a few other relatives wore or needed hearing aids. It was no surprise to the family when Marianne, at the age of 30, began to lose her hearing. For Marianne however, it proved to be a terrible blow. Even though she was already a teacher of the deaf, the idea of wearing hearing aids and using an interpreter in certain settings was foreign and frightening. Denial became the key to her survival. In the last few years, however, a Marianne has become a passionate advocate (some would say much too intense) for the rights and acceptance of Hard of Hearing people.

**Hampton School District**

**Marianne Rolling**
*Program Manager for the Hearing Impaired*

(708) 695-5699

22 Mainstream Ave.      Hampton, OH

**Edward Epson (E.E.), Production Supervisor**

Edward Epson (E.E.) as he is called by his friends, was born to Ellen and Alfred Epson, speech pathologists in practice together. E.E's deafness was discovered when he was two years old. At the time they discovered his hearing loss, Ellen and Alfred began to participate in a study using Cued Speech. They began diligently using it with their son. At the time they vowed that Edward would learn to speak and never learn sign. Both parents fought for the rights of their deaf son at a time before PL 94-142. Eventually Ellen left the practice and cued for her son full time. Edward is 40 years old and lives with his parents. He works at a small publishing house as a production supervisor. E.E. just finished his first semester of ASL.

**SHAW PUBLISHING**

Specializing in Special Interests

230 Curiosity Circle, Storey, TX 1244

Edward Epson, BS
Production Supervisor

(346) 887-5400 (V-TDD) (346) 887-5401 FAX

# TARGET RANGE

## ASK THE EXPERTS

### BIOGRAPHIES

**Joanne Lawrence, PhD**

Joanne is Deaf. Strong Deaf. She grew up in a family of Deaf people and has known family and community strength. For her, the only language of the deaf is ASL. She has worked for many years studying ASL and making a strong case for Bilingual/Bicultural education of the deaf. Joanne is currently a professor of linguistics. She also lectures on various topics related to Deafness in her spare time.

> **JOANNE LAWRENCE, Ph.D.**
>
> *Professor of Linguistics*
> Boston University
> 455 N. Modal Ave.
> Boston, MA 23566
>
> (408) 465-9822 ext. 87 (TDD)

**Patrice Vickers, Artistic Director**

Patrice is Deaf. She grew up in the midwest where she attended The Sunnyside Oral School for the Deaf. Bernice Jacobs was her teacher. Patrice was able to attend the oral school for only one year. Her family then moved to New Jersey where Patrice was enrolled in a mainstream program near her home. Patrice has strong opinions about what interpreters should and should not do in an educational setting! After receiving her degree from Gallaudet University, she pursued a career in acting. While she was a successful actress with the National Theatre of the Deaf, she felt drawn to managing theatre companies instead.

> **EAST COAST THEATRE OF THE DEAF**
>
>  2900 Lincoln Blvd.
> Thespian, NJ 00987
>
> *Patrice Vickers*
> artistic director
> (807) 455-8675 (V/TTY)

**Ted Kanhelp, MD**

Ted grew as the only hearing child in his family. With two deaf parents and two older deaf sisters Ted often felt different and lonely. He retreated to his books and spent many isolated hours reading alone in the attic. Ted began to interpret for his parents and sisters at a very young age. He feels as though he was forced to grow up too soon and he resents that. Ted often dreamed of the day when he could make his parents and his sisters hear.

> **TED KANHELP, MD**
> cochlear implant specialist
>
>
>
> 6599 Insert Ave, Recovery, AL
> (800) CAN-HEAR

# TARGET RANGE

## ASK THE EXPERTS

### BIOGRAPHIES

**Susie Moore, MSW**

Susie spent her college years knowing that she wanted to become a counselor. She always wanted to help any unfortunate soul. After receiving her Master's Degree she had a tough time finding a job. Finally, she heard of one in Indiana. She applied and was hired. The only trouble was...it involved working with deaf-mutes. Susie has no sign language experience and had never met a deaf-mute until she stared working. Bernice Jacobs has taken Susie under her wing and is offering lots of advice on how to deal with the hearing impaired.

INDIANA STATE SERVICES FOR THE HEARING IMPAIRED

Susie Moore, MSW Counselor

34 Redtape Ave, Theraputic, IN 46953
(317) 978-3455 (voice only)

**Bernice Jacobs, Principal**

Bernice is a staunch oralist. She believes that only hearing people should teach the hearing impaired. She does not subscribe to the notion that a deaf culture exists. She pities the poor hearing impaired people who do not fit into the mainstream of society. If a student does not learn to speak and speechread at her school, she considers it a personal failure. While some people may think that she is misguided, she is dedicated and fervent in her beliefs. She and Dr. Kanhelp are close friends.

**SUNNYDAY SCHOOL**

1200 Missedit Avenue
Sayagain, FL
(200) 666-9000

**Bernice Jacobs,** Principal
We Give the Hearing Impaired the Gift of Speech

# TARGET RANGE

## ASK THE EXPERTS

### BIOGRAPHIES

**Robin VanWert, Sign Language Interpreter (pre-cert.)**

Robin knew from the time that she was a young girl that she should become involved with the Deaf. She was always fascinated by sign and couldn't wait to learn it. Robin attended a two-year interpreter training program in Illinois. She graduated with flying colors. She adheres to the code of ethics passionately. Interestingly though, although she understands the idea that ASL is the language of the Deaf, she secretly believes that Signed English is the answer to the education of Deaf children. Her aunt was one of the original parents who helped develop Signed English. She grew up with conversations around the dinner table about the reading levels and language lags of Deaf children. Signed English just makes sense for her, while ASL does not.

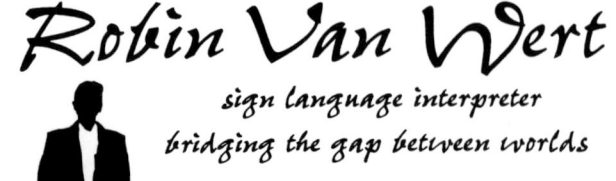

**Jason Probsky, Publisher**

Jason was deafened at the age of 12 by meningitis. His family was devastated and still have not come to grips with the fact that Jason is deaf. Because of Jason's love of reading and his experience with English as his first language, he decided to become a writer. His parents fronted the money for him to become the publisher of this small weekly magazine for Deaf people. Jason has strong opinions about how people learn language and why ASL should be the language of the Deaf. He also has some strong opinions about speechreading and oralism. Paradoxically, Jason recently underwent surgery for a cochlear implant. He has been surprised by the response from the Deaf community to him now.

# TARGET RANGE

## ASK THE EXPERTS
### Activity 1: Networking

**Practice Targets:** Numerals, Discourse, Structures, Articulation
**Level:** ★★
**Group Size:** Pairs
**Repeat:** Three times
**Materials:** Student Workbook pages 67, 68, 69, 70, 71, 72, 73, pencil
**Preparation:** There are three sets of Networking pages in the Student Workbook. Decide which set the students will complete.

**Background Information:** Each student has recently attended the biennial convention of the National Association of the Deaf. The convention was packed with fascinating people. Like many conventioneers, students exchanged business cards with people they met. Some of the information has been lost, however, a colleague might have most of the information for which the students are searching.

**Directions:** Pair students and assign them each a Workbook page. Explain that the information on the business cards on one Workbook page is related to the questions on the notebook page on the other Workbook page.

Each student will individually develop ASL questions based on the notes on the notebook on their Workbook page. When partners are ready, they will take turns asking and answering the questions they developed, and fill in the information they received.

# TARGET RANGE

## *ASK THE EXPERTS*
## Networking

**PAGE 68**

## *ASK THE EXPERTS*
## Networking

**PAGE 69**

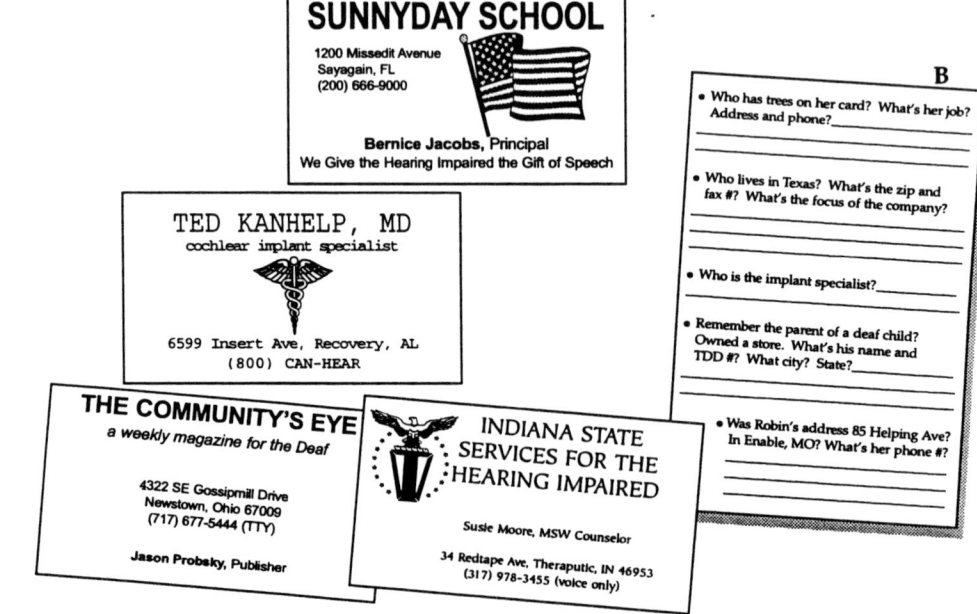

# TARGET RANGE

## *ASK THE EXPERTS*
## Networking

**PAGE 70**

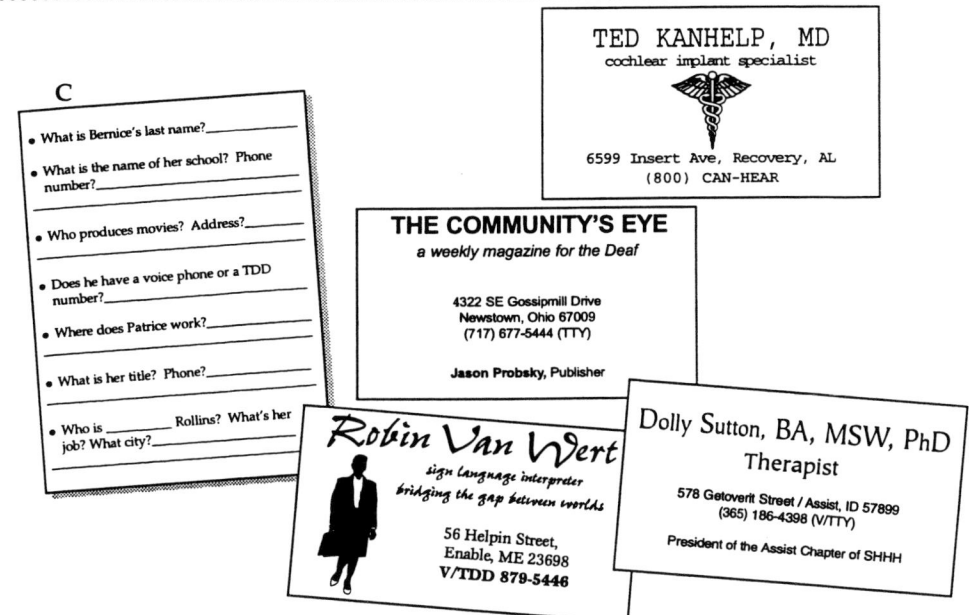

## *ASK THE EXPERTS*
## Networking

**PAGE 71**

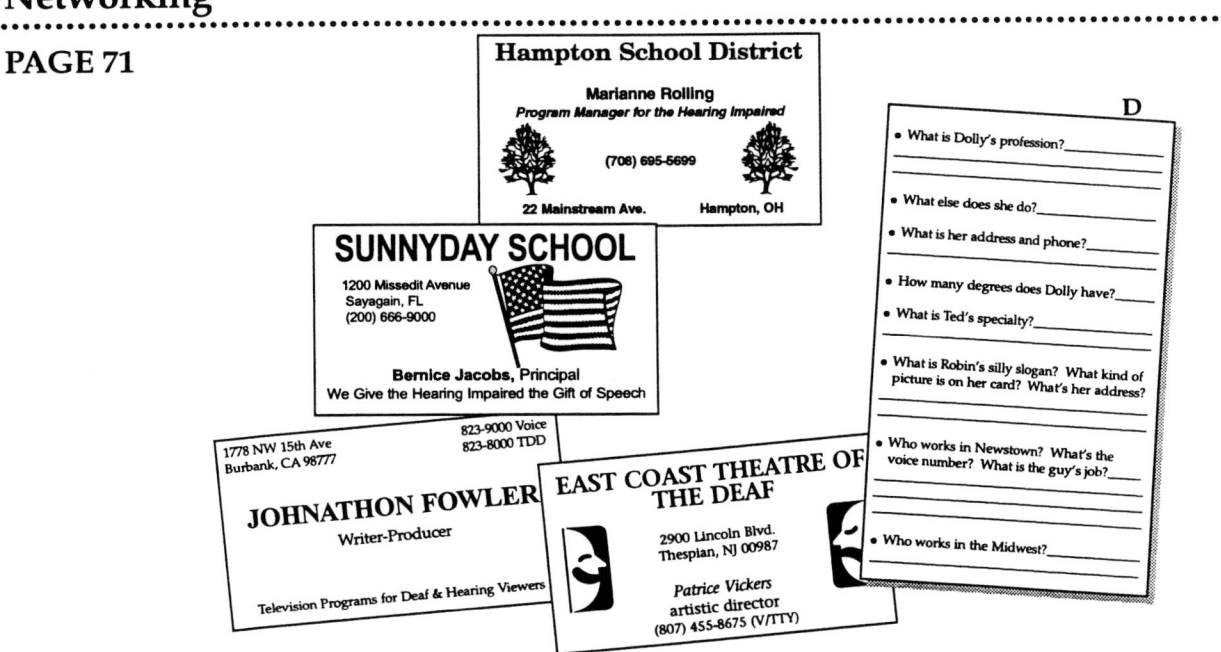

# TARGET RANGE

*ASK THE EXPERTS*
Networking

PAGE 72

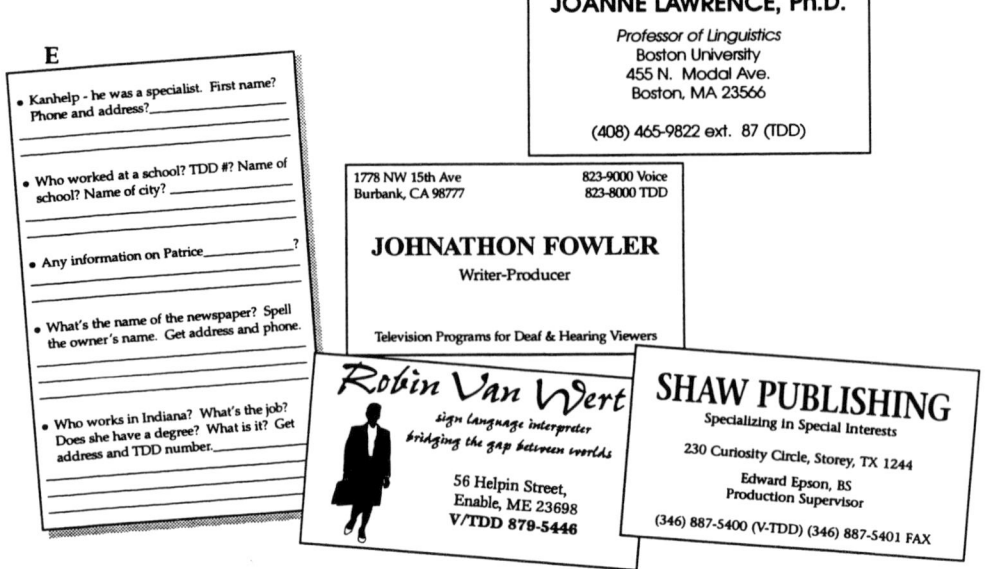

*ASK THE EXPERTS*
Networking

PAGE 73

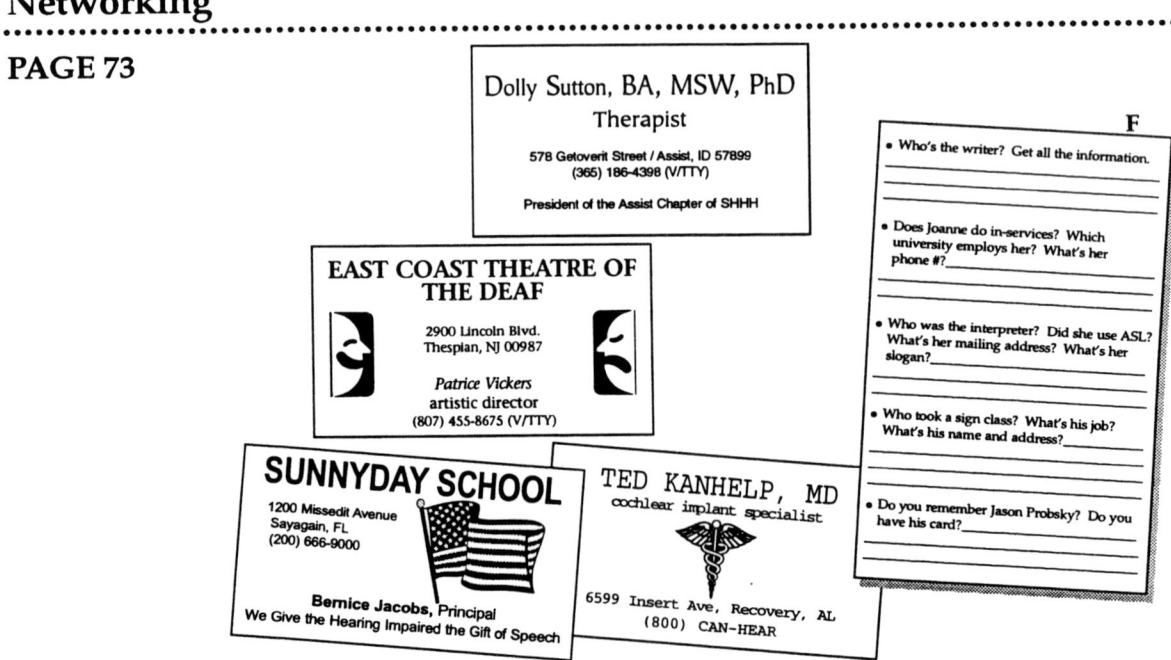

## TARGET RANGE

## ASK THE EXPERTS
### Activity 2: Panel Discussion

**Practice Targets:** Discourse, Structures, Articulation
**Level:** ★★★
**Group Size:** Large
**Repeat:** Yes
**Materials:** Student Workbook pages 74, 75, 12 Business Cards, 12 copies of the Student Directions
**Preparation:** Prior to the activity, choose 12 students. Copy the Student Directions, the biographies and business cards from the Teacher's Manual. Laminate the Business Cards if you choose. Distribute a card, a biography sheet and Student Directions to each student. On the day of the panel discussion, arrange the room so that the panel members can sit at the front of the room. Write the names of the participants on the board or provide name cards.

**Background Information:** Twelve community members involved with the Deaf have been asked to serve as panel members for a discussion about issues facing the Deaf Community. The location is the Hampton Center for the Deaf and Hard of Hearing.

**Directions:**
**The day before:**
Inform the class that there will be a panel discussion tomorrow. Those chosen to be panel members will discuss topics of interest to the Deaf Community. Audience members will question the panel members.

Choose 12 students to participate in this role play discussion. Give each student a business card, a biography and the directions. Instruct each panel member to read all the information about the characters in order to develop their own character.

**The day of the discussion:**
Prepare an area for the panel members. Inform the remaining students in the class that their role today is that of an eager audience member. Audience members will develop questions based on the notes on the Workbook page.

# TARGET RANGE

## ASK THE EXPERTS
**Student Directions**

You have been chosen to participate as a character in a panel discussion. You will be given a business card and a biography of the character you will play. As in any role play activity it is important to develop characters with some depth. Maintaining the character's personality during role play activities is also an important aspect.

To prepare for this role play activity read your character's biography. Take some time to consider what kind of life that charater has, his/her attitudes, philosophies, mannerisms, and views on the world. Sometimes a small idiosyncrasy can aid in the development of a character. Develop your opinions based on the character's biography and what you believe that character might say.

Prior the panel discussion your classmates will spend time developing questions for you based on the information on the workbook page. Take some time to look at the page and begin to develop a framework for your answers.

On the day of the panel discussion panel members will sit in a special area of the room and classmates will pose their questions.

# TARGET RANGE

## *ASK THE EXPERTS*
### Activity 2: Panel Discussion

Each member will choose from the various responses of the panel members and record one answer on the Workbook page. Students may choose to record the most interesting response or the most controversial response. They may also simply write down the first response to each question or choose one panel member and record his/her answers.

Begin the panel discussion by asking members to identify themselves and give some background information. Students in the audience can then form questions which will hopefully lead to a vigorous discussion.

**Note:** It may be helpful for students to have an opportunity to "de-brief" following the panel discussion. Important issues related to the topics, such as culture conflict, language issues and attitudes are likely to surface during the panel discussion. As you view the proceedings record issues you would like to address later. Look for the behaviors/usage/attitudes exhibited by students which impressed and or concerned you.

### REPLICA OF *PANEL DISCUSSION* FROM STUDENT WORKBOOK - PAGE 75

| Panel Member's Name: | Student's Name: _____ |
|---|---|
| _____ | 1. Background: Family _____ |
| _____ | 2. Work: _____ |
| _____ | 3. Feelings about cultural minority status of Deaf _____ |
| _____ | 4. Feelings about Bilingual/Bicultural education: _____ |
| _____ | 5. "Pet Peeve:" _____ |
| _____ | 6. Life Goals: _____ |
| _____ | 7. Ideal Deaf World: _____ |

107

# TARGET RANGE

## ASK THE EXPERTS
### Activity 3: Student Interview

**Practice Targets:** Structures, Discourse, Articulation
**Level:** ★★★
**Group Size:** Pairs
**Repeat:** No
**Materials:** Student Workbook pages 76, 77, pencil, *Ask the Experts Business Cards*
**Preparation:** Copy enough business cards so that each student will have one

**Background Information:** Students in a sign language class have requested interviews with some of the people who served on the panel discussion held at the Hampton Center for the Deaf and Hard of Hearing. Students have been assigned to complete an interview of a panel member.

**Directions:** Distribute a business card to each student. Pair students. Instruct teams to turn to the Workbook page. Assign the *professional* role to one of the partners. Allow the *professional* time to develop the character. Instruct the *professional* to carefully consider how his character would answer questions about various topics.

Assign the role of *student* to the other partner. Instruct the *student* to develop questions related to the information on the Workbook page. Encourage the *student* to carefully consider the personality characteristics of the *professional* being interviewed.

When partners are ready, the *student* can begin the interview by asking questions and then recording the information on the Workbook page. When the interview is completed the partners will reverse roles.

**Note:** Even though some of the characters are hearing, the interviews will be conducted using ASL. (You may choose not to include the character of Bernice Jacobs. As a staunch oralist she may not know sign language, or perhaps she does. Did she have a deaf relative?)

### REPLICA OF *STUDENT INTERVIEW* FROM STUDENT WORKBOOK - PAGE 77

Student's Name _____ Professional's Name _____

1. Background Information _____

2. Description of important issues facing his/her profession _____

3. Feelings about cochlear implants in children _____

4. Feelings about Deaf Culture _____

5. Feelings about mainstreaming vs. residential schools for the Deaf _____

6. One thing the ADA has done for him/her _____

# TARGET RANGE

## ASK THE EXPERTS
### Activity 4: Cocktail Party

**Practice Targets:** Discourse, Structures, Articulation
**Level:** ★★★
**Group Size:** Large
**Repeat:** Yes
**Materials:** A business card for each student, nametags
(Optional: food, beverages, plates, etc and costumes to add to the realism)
**Preparation:** Make enough copies of the cards so that each student has one card. Prepare nametags. Create areas for the various cocktail parties to occur in the room. Bring costumes and arrange for food.

**Background Information:** The recently opened Hampton Community Center for the Deaf and Hard of Hearing has become the new home for social services, the arts, and an interpreter referral service. The guests at this cocktail party are attending the Opening Gala.

The center is located in a downtown area which has recently seen a great deal of renovation. Since it is near bus routes, it is easily accessible. There are several very large offices and a spacious meeting room. This center has been a goal for many people for many years. Some people have worked long and hard for this center; other people have vehemently opposed the center, questioning the need for such programs.

**Directions:** Distribute a business card to each student. Assign each group of twelve students to a specific area in the room. Instruct students to read their own character description and the descriptions of the other community members who have been invited to this cocktail party. Allow time for students to develop a character for the role play.

Describe the role play guidelines to the students. Encourage students to generate lively discussions and debates about issues facing the Deaf community, just as they might at a real cocktail party.

# TARGET RANGE

## *ASK THE EXPERTS*
**Activity 4: Cocktail Party continued**

Possible topics for cocktail party discussion:

1. The ADA
2. The location of the Hampton Community Center for the Deaf and Hard of Hearing
3. Bilingual/Bicultural issues
4. How the center will be helpful for the Deaf community
5. The Hampton community's reaction to the center
6. Issues facing Deaf consumers with regards to interpreters
7. Accessibility issues
8. Cochlear implants for adults and children
9. Providing Deaf role models for deaf children of hearing parents
10. Mainstreaming programs vs. residential programs

# TARGET RANGE

## ASK THE EXPERTS
### Activity 5: Project 580/Deaf Studies

**Practice Targets:** Discourse, Structures, Articulation
**Level:** ★★★★
**Group Size:** Small
**Repeat:** No
**Materials:** Student Workbook pages 78, 79, pencil, business card for each student
**Preparation:** Copy and cut out the business cards

**Background Information:** Students are enrolled in a graduate school class entitled "Project 580/Deaf Studies." The final evaluation for the class will be based on a project. The project must demonstrate that people from various backgrounds and strong philosophies can still come together and find a common ground while creating something that is beneficial to the Deaf and hearing communities alike. Project teams will proceed as though finances will not be a problem.

### Part I  The Discussions
**Directions:** Distribute a business card to each student. Assign students to small groups. Allow students an opportunity to create a character for the role play activity. The activity will end in a presentation of the group project.

Over the next several days allow time for groups to meet and generate ideas for their final project. Encourage teams to look at individual strengths and talents rather than philosophies. Consensus and compromise will become important as they look at various project ideas which benefit their community.

Depending on the level of the students, this project can become very complicated. Because the dynamics of each group of characters is different, each group's project will represent a unique blending of their specialties and skills.

As each group develops their project, they can fill in the Student Workbook page.

# TARGET RANGE

## ASK THE EXPERTS
### Activity 5: Project 580/Deaf Studies

**Part II**   **The Presentations**

Once a group has reached consensus and decided on a project, instruct them to use the Student Workbook page to fill in the details. Groups can then begin the process of developing a 10 minute presentation which describes their project. Encourage creativity, vision, as well as a dose of reality.

Each presentation should include the information on the Workbook page as well as the following:

1. Introduction of each character involved in the Project
2. Each character should briefly discuss in writing or ASL why s/he believes this project will benefit the community and how the project is able to mesh with their individual philosophy
3. A discussion of the process they used to reach consensus
4. A description of the conflicts which occurred during their meetings
5. Any insights they have

**REPLICA OF *PROJECT 580/DEAF STUDIES* FROM STUDENT WORKBOOK - PAGE 79**

---

PROJECT 580/DEAF STUDIES

Project Title:_____   _____Projected Cost:_____

Team member names: _____   _____   _____   _____

Goal/Purpose of Project:
_____
_____
_____
_____

Description of project including how it affects the Deaf community, how it will happen, who will be involved, when it will happen, and how it blends each of the team members' specific interests and philosophies.
_____
_____
_____
_____
_____
_____
_____
_____

# TARGET RANGE

## *NONE OF YOUR BUSINESS*

All of the activities in *None of Your Business* involve creating characters and role play. Many of these activities are open-ended. Mirroring real life, partners or groups will determine the course of the conversations.

Unlike *Ask the Experts*, students will not be offered character descriptions. Instead, they will have the opportunity to create, from the inside out, a persona for each of the activities to follow.

For these activities to be of most benefit, it is important that students create characters with some depth and maintain those character attributes during role play. Encourage students to take some time to consider what kind of life that character has, attitudes, philosophies, mannerisms, views on the world, idiosyncrasies, etc. Sometimes a bit of a costume will add to the fun. If the business card has a name on it, students will assume that persona. If the business card does not have a name on it, students will need to invent a name.

## *NONE OF YOUR BUSINESS*
**Business Cards**

**BIKE REPAIR**
Bob's Bike Repair
12 Speedy Lane • Antioch, Michigan
(800) 499-5555

*ILLUSIONS DRESS SHOPPE*
what you see is what you get
**(800) 426-6833**
we specialize in
hard to fit sizes
16 Barrit Ave          Disappearing, OH

(800) 866-2442

eprechan Financial Services

Patrick O'Callahan, Proprietor
123 Rainbow Lane          Magic, Texas
*we'll make magic for a wee big o' green*

Fiona's Fancy Fireworks

911 Call St.
Boomtown, Mass.
(800) 222-9111

*stop by our
remodeled showroom
it's a blast from the past!*

# TARGET RANGE

## NONE OF YOUR BUSINESS
Business Cards

---

### Jacque's Bistro
*we serve it up family style*

222-4000

1111 S. Main    Tupelo, Idaho

---

### AL'S DISCOUNT CHEMICALS
**better living through chemistry**

4321 Blastoff Lane/Deadsoon, OK
**(987) 654-3210**

---

### SPARKY'S AUTORAMA
just West of I44 in Eastville
Westwood, SC    544-8634

"if it's got some spark...
come see ol' Sparky for a trade in!"

---

3354 Sashimi Way    Ichi, Ohio    867-4476

### ¥AKAMOTO'S IMPORTS

*"when you yen for that oriental flair"*

---

### MOM'S LONG HAUL TRUCKING
321 Homewood Ave    Cookinggood, GA
(800) 677- 9977

*and you know how particular MOM is!*

---

### Radicals Against Gas Emissions
a non-profit group working for you

556 Bean Blvd. Suite B    Toot, MO
**557-8974**
**together we can prevent gas pollution**

---

### LONELY PINES RESORT
R.R. 3 Lonely Lake Rd
Lonely Lake, ID
(800) 666-4144

• skiing • fishing • golf

*"we're pining away for you..."*

---

### CITY REALTY
132 Main St.    Eastport, NY
(800) 455-3889

• apartments • homes • duplexes
• businesses • bridges

# TARGET RANGE

## NONE OF YOUR BUSINESS
Business Cards

---

### Mac Donald Real Estate

RR 5 Old Hwy 44

**233-9900**

*specializing in agriculture and livestock*

---

### Home Town Brewery

**Billy & Joe Bob Brewster**
**Rural Route 6, Old Hwy 17**
**346-6809**

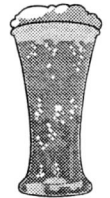

*come on in for a free taste - we use the freshest hops from our Daddy's crops*

---

### monique's auto salvage

**19987 Old Muffler Hwy**
**Exhaust, MO 980-3465**

**"wrecking with a woman's touch"**

---

### COMP-U-SHOP

your self-serve computer store

10101 Hwy 111   Dos, MS
**(800) 101-0011**

*if we don't know it,*
*we don't show it!*

---

### EXCELLENT EXCAVATING

14111 E. Level Lane   Clearlake, MI

| 769-0097 |
| free estimates gladly! |

We do all types of dozer work
but we don't sleep on the job!

---

### ROCKY'S FROZEN YOGURT

top floor at the mall
at birthdays - we're a knock-out!

• Specialty ice cream cakes
• 13 different toppings
• waffle cones
**677-0090**

---

*To be buried — you know it's their last request*

### DOORNALE FUNERAL HOME

3000 Deadwood Parkway
Heavenly, CO

**556-6788**

---

### The Fruit Farm

*Old Huckleberry Rd*
*Crabapple Cove, VT*
*899-0043*

*our fruit is fresh, but our clerks aren't!*

# TARGET RANGE

## *NONE OF YOUR BUSINESS*
### Business Cards

---

**TOPS 'N BOTTOMS**
exclusively for men

1715 Hattrick Ave.
Hatteras, NJ
332-8998

we fit your budget even if it's on a shoestring!

---

**Wrong Turn Employment Agency**

768 N.E. Add Blvd.   Nohope, Al
**(800) 555-7788**

*"The road to success starts here!"*

---

**SKIP'S BASEBALL MEMORABELIA**

*for those of us who never grew up!*

- baseball cards
- autographed balls
- rare and unusual items
- Topps cards
- Donruss
- Fleer

Visa & MasterCard accepted
**800-455-9800**

---

*the cheese factory*

4600 Brie Blvd.         Camebembert, KY

- cheddars  ■ Jack  ■ Swiss
- our own special Limburger

"I KNOW CHEESE!"
Mick M. Ouse, Proprietor

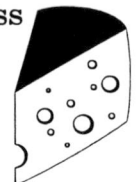

---

**NOREEGA DISCOUNT DRUGS**

6000 Sky High Drive      Outlaw, Tx.

*we specialize in hard to find medicines*

open 24 hours
**900-778-9000**

*franchises available for enterprizing folks*

---

**Dr. Mor E. Payne**

*If you're afraid of anethesia, see me!*

**677-2443**

*new patients welcome!*

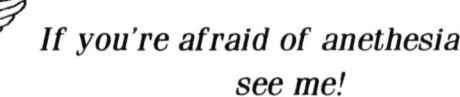

---

**LEGIT BUSINESS BUREAU**
443 Strait St.      Normal, IL

**800-888-7000**

we got the power
to test 'em and arrest 'em

---

*SALLY'S SPORTING GOODS*

3449 Shortstop Rd.    Battonball, WA

**694-8677**

we only sell to good sports

# TARGET RANGE

## NONE OF YOUR BUSINESS
**Business Cards**

**TYPEWRITERS BY ANTONIO**
112 Corona Lane   Writer, PA
(800) 333-0977

**STAR STRUCK DANCE STUDIO**

5536 Footloose St.
Boots, Or.
469-7787

we can-can make you a star!

**KRIS KRINGLE RECYCLING**

used trees for cash
1000 Reindeer Dr.
North Pole
(800) 222-4669

"we're checking our list"

**Marnie's Discount Make-Up**
414 Shadow St.  Coverd, Vt
**449-7778**
* BEAUTY MAKE-OVERS
* BODY WRAPS

with our prices,
you'll really make out!
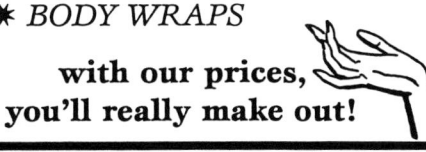

**illusions magic shoppe**
1000 Secrecy Ave.
Kalamazoo, Mi
555-8871

come in for a hare raising experience

"we're always on the cutting edge"
**SAM'S SCISSOR SHARPENING SHOP**

228 Bledsoe Blvd.
256-2336

# TARGET RANGE

## NONE OF YOUR BUSINESS
### Activity 1: An Evening of Amateur Mime

**Practice Targets:** Readiness
**Level:** ★
**Group Size:** Large
**Repeat:** Yes
**Materials:** Student Workbook pages 81, 82, a trophy to represent the *Oscar*, *None of Your Business* business cards (Optional: Costumes)
**Preparation:** Copy and laminate the business cards, find the *Oscar*, clear a space in the room for the pantomime activities.

**Background Information:** The Better Business Bureau is sponsoring a fundraising event for the Hampton Food Shelves. *An Evening of Amateur Mime* offers local business owners an opportunity to advertise their services in a different way.

**Directions:** For *An Evening of Amateur Mime* each student will create a solo pantomime skit which will advertise one or more of their businesses' products or services. Students will take turns performing. When not performing, students will serve as audience members.

Distribute a business card to each student. Instruct them to keep the identity a secret. Discuss and demonstrate the creation of a character, role play guidelines, and the invention of a name if necessary. Allow time for each student to create a character based on the business card.

Inform students that each skit should be done strictly in pantomime, performed alone and last for at least one minute.

When each student is ready, arrange the room so that there is an area for performance. Determine the order of performers. List businesses which will be represented on the board if you choose. Inform students that they will try to guess the business and/or product that the each performer is trying to sell.

Instruct audience members (any student not performing) to use the Workbook page to help them record their guesses and keep track of the performers and their businesses.

# TARGET RANGE

## *NONE OF YOUR BUSINESS*
### Activity 1: An Evening of Amateur Mime

When the skits are finished, convene as a class and compare answers. Vote on the most creative skit and award that student with the *Oscar*.

**Notes:**
1. Costumes really make this activity come alive! Real audience members add to the thrills, as do real judges. Find students from other classes to sit in as judges for the skits.
2. It is helpful to record the business names on the board.
3. Students can bring cans of food to donate to local food shelves.
4. You may choose to do this activity over two days. One half of the class will perform on one day while the other half serves as audience members. The next day the roles will be reversed.

## REPLICA OF *AN EVENING OF AMATEUR MIME* FROM STUDENT WORKBOOK - PAGE 82

| Business: | Business: | Business: | Business: | Business: | Business: |
|---|---|---|---|---|---|
| Selling: | Selling: | Selling: | Selling: | Selling: | Selling: |
| Business: | Business: | Business: | Business: | Business: | Business: |
| Selling: | Selling: | Selling: | Selling: | Selling: | Selling: |
| Business: | Business: | Business: | Business: | Business: | Business: |
| Selling: | Selling: | Selling: | Selling: | Selling: | Selling: |

# TARGET RANGE

## *NONE OF YOUR BUSINESS*
### Activity 2: Chamber of Commerce Meeting

**Practice Targets:** Discourse, Structures, Articulation
**Level:** ★★★
**Group Size:** Large
**Repeat:** Yes
**Materials:** Student Workbook pages 83, 84, 85, *None of Your Business* business cards
**Preparation:** Have business cards ready for distribution
(Optional: bring costumes and arrange for snacks and beverages)

**Background Information:** This gathering represents the first meeting of the new Hampton Chamber of Commerce. The Hampton community has never been organized enough to get something like this started. In fact, many of the business owners have never socialized with each other. It is no surprise that they don't know much about each others' businesses.

**Directions:** Distribute a business card to each student. Discuss and demonstrate the creation of a character, role play guidelines and the invention of a name if necessary. Allow time for each student to create a character based on the business card. For this activity instruct each student to decide upon at least one unique hobby their character enjoys or an unusual kind of service they provide. For example, the funeral director may be a hairdresser on the side or the person selling sporting goods may have a hobby of tying flies for fly fishing.

While the students are developing their characters, take a moment and assume the character of the newly elected Mayor of Hampton. Since this is the first meeting of the group, begin with a short ad-libbed speech. When each student has developed a character and a hobby, meet together to begin the meeting.

**Note:** Don't worry if there are business cards left over. Those cards can represent business owners who did not attend the meeting.

# TARGET RANGE

## NONE OF YOUR BUSINESS
Activity 2: Chamber of Commerce Meeting

**REPLICA OF *CHAMBER OF COMMERCE MEETINGS* FROM STUDENT WORKBOOK - PAGES 84, 85**

| CHAMBER OF COMMERCE MEETING ||||||
|---|---|---|---|---|---|
| NAME | BUSINESS | HOBBY/SERVICE | NAME | BUSINESS | HOBBY/SERVICE |
| Realtor | | | Scissor Shop Owner | | |
| Resort Owner | | | Real Estate Broker | | |
| Dress Shop Owner | | | Dance Instructor | | |
| Yogurt Shop Owner | | | Typewriter Shop | | |
| Card Shop Owner | | | Fruit Farm Owner | | |
| Haberdasher | | | Brewery Owner | | |
| Dentist | | | Chemical Warehouse | | |
| Funeral Director | | | Restaurant Owner | | |

| CHAMBER OF COMMERCE MEETING ||||||
|---|---|---|---|---|---|
| NAME | BUSINESS | HOBBY | NAME | BUSINESS | HOBBY |
| Cheese Shop Owner | | | Militant Citizen | | |
| Trucker | | | Employment Agency | | |
| Importer | | | Auto Salvage | | |
| Computer Store Owner | | | Bike Repair | | |
| Car Salesman | | | Financier | | |
| Magician | | | Excavator | | |
| Fireworks Owner | | | Recycler | | |
| Business Bureau | | | Beauty Consultant | | |
| Sporting Goods Owner | | | Discount Drug Owner | | |

# TARGET RANGE

## *NONE OF YOUR BUSINESS*
### Activity 3: Errands

**Practice Targets:** Discourse, Structures, Articulation
**Level:** ★★★
**Group Size:** Large
**Repeat:** Yes
**Materials:** Student Workbook pages 86, 87, a *None of Your Business* business card for each student, construction paper for signs, copies of the Errands cut into strips, pencil (Optional: Costumes & props for store owners)
**Preparation:** Copy the business cards, make enough copies of the Errands and cut them into strips so that each student has several. Arrange the room so that there is a place for the students to mingle and a place for the owners to set up shop.

**Background Information:** Everyone in Hampton is attending the first Hampton Saturday Market. People are milling around looking at the hand-crafted items and farm produce. They are also catching up on what's been happening in town over the winter. This setting provides a perfect opportunity for business owners to see each other and take care of some of their own errands.

**Directions:** Divide the class into thirds. Distribute a business card to each student. Inform one third of the class that they will be shop owners who are displaying their wares at the Hampton Saturday Market. Provide two errand strips to each business owner working Saturday Market.

Give several errand strips to each student in the other two thirds of the class. Allow time for students to develop characters, make the signs for their businesses and become familiar with their errands.

When the class is ready and the businesses are set up, students will visit the businesses, chat, do their errands and fill in the Student Workbook page. Saturday Market business owners will either be lucky and complete their errands or not.

## REPLICA OF *ERRANDS* FROM STUDENT WORKBOOK - PAGE 87

| Errand purpose: _____ | Errand purpose: _____ |
|---|---|
| Business name: _____ | Business name: _____ |
| Employee name: _____ | Employee name: _____ |
| Address: _____ Phone: _____ | Address: _____ Phone: _____ |
| Slogan: _____ | Slogan: _____ |
| Meeting when? _____ | Meeting when? _____ |

# TARGET RANGE

## *NONE OF YOUR BUSINESS*
### Activity 3: Errands

**ERRANDS**

---

Find a Realtor. You are thinking about selling your house and you want that person to give you an appraisal at 4:00 next Thursday. Be sure to find out three of the Realtor's specialties.

---

You have to stop off at the brewery and talk with one of the owners about scheduling a tour for your cousin's Girl Scout Troop. You can't come on Tuesdays or Thursdays. Saturday afternoons are not good either.

---

You need to order some baseball cards for your Dad's 50th birthday next month. You want to order a 1962 Post Cereal complete set. Don't pay over $745.00. Be sure it is a complete set—your Dad really loves Ernie Banks.

---

You have to stop by the Cheese Factory today to pick up some of their newest Limburger cheese. Find out when it will be ready. Ask the owner if he is any relation to Minny.

---

You have had a craving for tuti-fruiti frozen yogurt. Talk to the owner about whipping you up a waffle cone. Find out about his background. What did he do before he was in the yogurt business?

---

Your grandma really loves red raspberry jam from the Fruit Farm. Ask the owner if she will sell you 7 quarts of the jam and find out the cost.

---

Your typewriter is broken. The parenthesis sticks to the paper. Find the repair shop owner. What is his motto?

---

You have always wanted to take dance lessons and recently won free lessons from the Star Struck Studio. Talk with the owner and find out if she has trained any famous dancers. Find out the price of regular lessons (in case you want to continue later) and where the studio is located.

# TARGET RANGE

## *NONE OF YOUR BUSINESS*
### Activity 3: Errands

**ERRANDS**

> You and your family are longing to get away for the weekend. You want to travel to Idaho to see the famous Tater Museum. Find someone who owns an Inn. See when they have room for your family of seven. How much will that cost for a weekend?

> You are thinking of selling your small farm. There are several Realtors in town, but you want someone who specializes in farms. Find out the owner's name and how he got into the real estate business.

> The 4th of July is coming up and you are preparing for a large party. Of course it would not be complete without fireworks. Check with Fiona and find out the prices of her most fancy fireworks. See if she will deliver them for free. Be sure to keep her phone number.

> You are a chemist and you are looking for some chemicals for your own personal experiments. Find someone willing to sell you chemicals for a cheap price. Be sure to get the name and address. Check with the Legit Business Bureau to find out if the business is legitimate.

> You are looking for someone to sharpen some old scissors your grandmother had. They are quite rusty but you think they will sharpen fine. Get the address of a shop and talk to the owner about that. Find out what his slogan is.

> You are looking for a magician for your niece's next birthday party. Find someone who knows something about magic and see if you can hire a magician. The party is Saturday the 7th of next month at 4:00 in the afternoon. Be sure to ask about the slogan.

# TARGET RANGE

## *NONE OF YOUR BUSINESS*
**Activity 3: Errands**

### ERRANDS

Your widowed aunt from California died and left you quite a bit of her antique furniture. The furniture brings back fond memories of your childhood. Find a trucking company that will transport the furniture to you. Be sure you find someone you trust. Write down the phone number.

Your car broke down between Eastville and Westwood. Find someone to repair it for you. You amy want to talk about trading in your old pile of junk for a new car. Get the slogan of the business and remember to write down the phone number. (You may want to check with the Legit Business Bureau.)

Your goldfish just died and you don't want to give it a wet funeral. You were friends for a long time and you want the memorial service to be a special one. Find someone who will help you plan a funeral for your fish. Find out if that city is close to yours. What kind of plan can you work out if the city is far from yours?

You are looking for a computer for yourself. Find a company representative and ask him to recommend a specific type of computer for your needs. Be sure to write down the address and phone number of the business and the representative name.

You are a concerned citizen of Toot, Missouri. Your major gripe is all the gas emissions that are polluting the air. Find a representative from R.A.G.E. And find out what they stand for. Let the representative sell you on the organization. Find out what kinds of things they are doing in the community. Don't forget to write down their phone number along with the president's name.

# TARGET RANGE

## *NONE OF YOUR BUSINESS*
### Activity 3: Errands

**ERRANDS**

> Last year you visited Japan. You had a wonderful time and brought back many gifts. It appears however, that you neglected to bring back anything for dear Uncle Harold. Find Ms. Yakamoto and ask her to recommend something for your Uncle Harold. Be sure to write down the shop's name, address and phone number.

> Uncle Alfred's birthday is coming up next month. Since he will be moving to New York City soon, you want to buy him something that he will be able to wear in the city. We all know that Uncle Harold's sense of fashion is rooted in the 70's. Ask the salesperson of a men's store what would be good for a man like Uncle Alfred. Write down the address, phone number and slogan of the business.

> You were just fired from you job as a gardener. You are actually relieved about what happened because you don't like to work outside in the cold. Find someone who might give you a job or help you find suitable employment. You have some typing skills and you are really good with your hands. You can also cook a little.

> You are looking for a restaurant that can cater to a large family gathering. You want something somewhat elegant but reasonable. There will be 27 people including you at the dinner party. Try to set it up for Saturday night the 27th at 6:00. Find out the menu items and how much each dinner will cost. Does the restaurant provide vegetarian options? Is there an extra cost? Don't forget to get the owner's name and the phone number.

> You have some trees in your yard that you want cut. Find a service that will trim your trees. Be sure to check with the Legit Business Bureau to see if this business is on the level. In addition, get the tree service's phone number and address. Find out if they will pay you to haul the trees off your property.

# TARGET RANGE

## *NONE OF YOUR BUSINESS*
### Activity 3: Errands

**ERRANDS**

Your mother-in-law is coming from Maine. You are looking for a dress shop that she might enjoy visiting. She has rather particular tastes. Find someone who owns a dress shop and ask her about the styles. How much are larger-sized dresses? Find out the address of the store and its phone number.

You want to be a model but you don't have much money this month. Can you find a store that will sell you make-up at a reasonable price? Find out about their specials and, just for kicks, ask if there are any job openings.

Uncle Elmer died last winter and left you his Edsel. You don't know exactly what to do with it. For the time being, it is stored in your Dad's garage, but he wants you to get rid of it. Shop around and see if you can find someone who will pay you what it's worth. Check the salvage prices too.

Aunt Marcia left you several thousand dollars—just what you need to get the land you bought ready for your dream house! Look for someone who can take care of leveling the big hill that is on your property. Make an appointment for a bid. Find out their address, phone number and their motto. Check with the Legit Business Bureau and see if the company is recommended.

Your Aunt Dee is coming to visit. She is a bizarre old bird, to say the least. She always arrives with a butler to your small apartment. She also brings along her bird Kiester, who is a pain. And, she brings her three wheeled tricycle. She has sent you a cable from Africa informing you that the trike broke on her most recent safari. She wants you to find a shop which can repair her trike. Find out how much it will cost, how long it will take and if they will deliver the trike.

# TARGET RANGE

## *NONE OF YOUR BUSINESS*
### Activity 3: Errands

**ERRANDS**

> Your Uncle Garreth was a little old winzied Irishman. And a true Irishman he was. He loved his Irish stew and said that a meal was not a meal without a potato and a pint of grog. When poor Garreth passed on it was his wish to have an Irish wake. During that time, his will was read. You received a good sum of money but only on one condition. You have to find a man from Magic, Texas. Your Uncle Garreth said to give him all the money and your faith and then wait to see what happened. Among other things, you feel you should check with the Legit Business Bureau. Then, find out about this man. What is the name of his business? What is his motto? What's his phone number and address?

> Your long faithful hound Buster has been your constant companion since you were a youngster. Now that you've graduated from college, your parents have given you the dog as an "apartment warming" gift. You have seen the veterinarian and he recommends mega-doses of vitamins and pain killers. Locate a pharmacy and see if they have the drugs you need. Since you are newly graduated, talk to the person about job opportunities.

> You are new to the community of Filling, Oklahoma. You are in need of dental care. Find someone from Filling and ask about the quality of care there. Ask about the Doctor's school background and inquire about office hours. Don't forget to check with the Legit Business Bureau.

# TARGET RANGE

## *NONE OF YOUR BUSINESS*
### Activity 4: Roommate Wanted

**Practice Targets:** Discourse, Structures, Articulation
**Level:** ★★★
**Group Size:** Large
**Repeat:** Yes
**Materials:** Student Workbook pages 88, 89, a *None of Your Business* business card for each student, pencil (Optional: Costumes and props)
**Preparation:** Have business cards ready to distribute, arrange seating area

**Background Information:** The Hampton Realtors are sponsoring a seminar for apartment seekers entitled *People Matches*. One of the goals of the seminar is to teach people how to recognize different and varied personality traits, likes and dislikes. This activity is part of that seminar.

**Directions:** Distribute a business card to each student. Discuss and demonstrate the creation of a character, role play guidelines, and the invention of a name if necessary. Allow time for each student to create a character based on the business card.

Instruct half of the class to fill in one of the *Roommate Wanted* cards on the Student Workbook page as their characters would. Instruct the remaining students to fill in one of the *Want to Share an Apartment* cards as their characters would. Encourage students to imagine the kind of apartment or roommate their characters would want. When all of the students have filled in the cards, arrange the students so that the *Roommate Wanted* students sit facing the *Want to Share an Apartment* students.

A student holding a *Roommate Wanted* card begins by describing the apartment s/he has and the roommate he hopes to find. A student who holds a *Want to Share an Apartment* card can respond if such a living arrangement meets his needs. In an effort to access the compatibility of such a match, the *Roommate Wanted* student may ask the *Want to Share an Apartment* seeker to describe the information on the card.

# TARGET RANGE

## *NONE OF YOUR BUSINESS*
### Activity 4: Roommate Wanted

This type of exchange continues, back and forth among characters, until roommates are matched, or until it is apparent that no matches are available. Hopefully students who have apartments will find suitable roommates. Encourage students to improvise, ad-lib, and enjoy the search.

When students have agreed to share an apartment, they can move their chairs back so that it is obvious that they are not participating but can still see the discussions. Play continues until most of the participants have a roommate.

**Variations:**
1. **Mingle:** Instead of formally seating students, encourage them to mingle with each other in hopes of finding a match.
2. **Blind Ads:** Materials: Enough index cards so that each student will have one, tape or tacks and a bulletin board, pencil and paper for each student.

**Directions:** Do not distribute a business card to each student. Instead, assign each student a secret number. Record each student's secret number. On their index cards. Student will record the secret number and write a brief but accurate description of themselves and the real qualities they desire in a roommate.

Collect the index cards and mix them up. Post them on the bulletin board or make photocopies of the cards and distribute them to the students. Students will read the cards and write down the numbers and the descriptions of the characteristics on the cards which appeal most to them. Instruct students to choose the best three cards.

Reconvene as a group. One student will begin by describing the characteristics on one of the cards they chose. The student who recognizes those characteristics can come forward and identify himself. If no one comes forward, or more than one student steps forward, the student can use the secret number on the card which should be recognized. Continue the activity in this manner until everyone has found their three matches.

**3. My Mother's Roommate**
In this variation, students describe one of their parents and the qualities they would desire in a roommate. Follow the same procedure as in Blind Ads.

# TARGET RANGE

## *NONE OF YOUR BUSINESS*
### Activity 4: Roommate Wanted

**REPLICA OF *ROOMMATE WANTED* FROM STUDENT WORKBOOK - PAGE 89**

| **ROOMMATE WANTED:** | **ROOMMATE WANTED:** | **ROOMMATE WANTED:** |
|---|---|---|
| Desired Qualities: _____ _____ _____ _____ _____ See: _____ if you match this description | Desired Qualities: _____ _____ _____ _____ _____ See: _____ if you match this description | Desired Qualities: _____ _____ _____ _____ _____ See: _____ if you match this description |

| **WANTED TO SHARE APT.** | **WANTED TO SHARE APT.** | **WANTED TO SHARE APT.** |
|---|---|---|
| Apt. Description: _____ _____ _____ Roomate Qualities: _____ _____ See: _____ for more information. | Apt. Description: _____ _____ _____ Roomate Qualities: _____ _____ See: _____ for more information. | Apt. Description: _____ _____ _____ Roomate Qualities: _____ _____ See: _____ for more information. |

# TARGET RANGE

## *NONE OF YOUR BUSINESS*
**Activity 5: Help Wanted!**

**Practice Targets:** Discourse, Structures, Numerals, Articulation
**Level:** ★★★
**Group Size:** Pairs
**Repeat:** No
**Materials:** Student Workbook pages 90, 91, 92, pencil (Optional: Costumes)
**Preparation:** None

**Background Information:** Two friends are both in search of new careers, or at least interim jobs. Both of them are reading want ad sections of different newspapers.

**Directions:** Pair students. Assign Workbook pages to each partner. Instruct partners to study their want ads. When they are ready, students can discuss each of the job opportunities in each other's newspapers.

Instruct each student to choose three job opportunities from either of the Want Ad pages and record the necessary information on the Workbook page.

**Variations:**
**1. I've Lost My Job!**
**Materials:** *None of Your Business* business cards, Student Workbook page, paper and pencil
**Directions:** Distribute a business card to each student. Pair students and instruct them to develop a character based on the business card. Instruct students to assume that they are now unemployed. Students should choose the top three job opportunities based on their character's qualifications and record the pertinent information on paper.

**2. My Sister Needs a Job!**
**Materials:** Want Ads for each student, paper and pencil
**Directions:** Distribute the local newspaper Want Ads to each student. Pair students. Inform students that they are helping their sister look for a part time job. Students should choose the top three job opportunities based on their sister's qualifications and record the pertinent information on paper.

# TARGET RANGE

## NONE OF YOUR BUSINESS
### Activity 5: Help Wanted!

**REPLICA OF *HELP WANTED!* FROM STUDENT WORKBOOK - PAGES 91, 92**

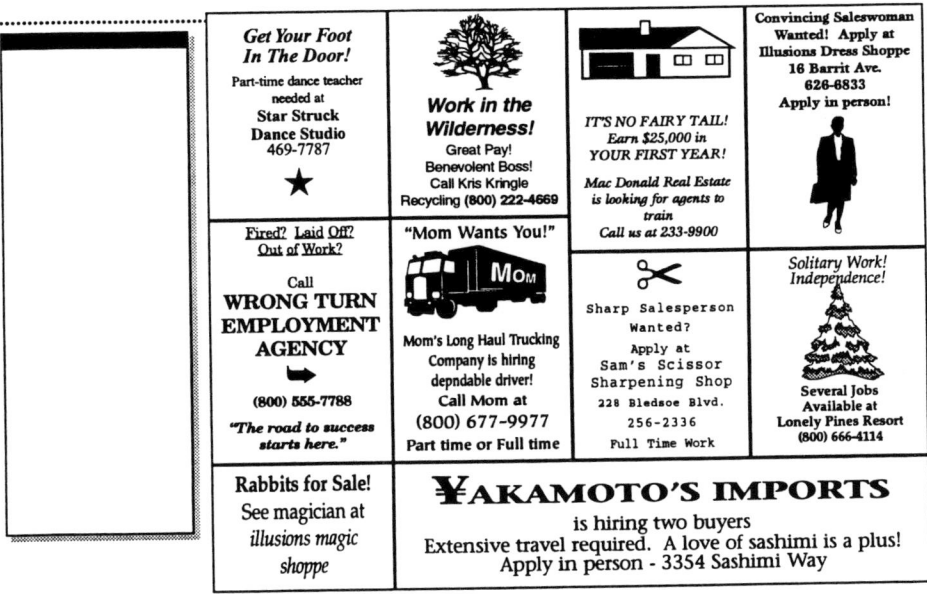

# TARGET RANGE

## *NONE OF YOUR BUSINESS*
**Activity 6: Interview!**

.................................................................................................................

**Practice Targets:** Discourse, Time, Structures, Articulation
**Level:** ★★★
**Group Size:** Large
**Repeat:** No
**Materials:** Student Workbook pages 93, 94, 95, *None of Your Business* business cards, pencil, construction paper and markers for business signs  (Optional: Costumes)
**Preparation:** Have business cards ready for distribution, arrange the classroom so that there is an area for each business for interviews

.................................................................................................................

**Background Information:** Students are *Job Seekers* participating in a Job Fair presented by the Hampton Chamber of Commerce.

**Directions:** Divide the class into thirds. One third of the students will become the *Employers*. Distribute a business card to each *Employer*. *Employers* will use the business card to create a character. The remaining two thirds of the class will become the *Job Seekers*. *Job Seekers* will have the freedom to create a character without the limits of a business card.

Discuss and demonstrate the creation of a character, role play guidelines, and the invention of a name if necessary. Allow time for each student to create their characters.

Instruct the *Employers* to turn to the appropriate page in the Student Workbook, create and fill in the necessary information. Inform them that they also need to create a business sign using the construction paper and markers.

Instruct the *Job Seekers* to use the Workbook page as a guide and create a resume based on their character.

Arrange the room so that the *Employers* will have an area in which they can interview the *Job Seekers*. Play begins when *Employers* and *Job Seekers* are ready.

# TARGET RANGE

## *NONE OF YOUR BUSINESS*
### Activity 6: Interview!

*Job Seekers*: will submit their resumes to prospective *Employers* and ask for an interview. During this process the *Employers* are expected to hire people, offer advice, or reject candidates. Each *Employer* must interview at least three *Job Seekers*. *Employers* will use the Student Workbook page to record the pertinent information about the people they interview. In order to be hired, a *Job Seeker* must meet at least one of the requirements for the *Employer's* position.

Play continues until most of the *Job Seekers* have found employment.

**Note:** To assist the *Job Seekers* write a list on the board of the *Employers* who are participating in the Job Fair.

---

## REPLICA OF *INTERVIEW! Employer's Page* FROM STUDENT WORKBOOK - PAGE 94

```
┌─────────────────────────────────┐  ┌─────────────────────────────────┐
│ Business Name: _____  │  │          Applicant #1           │
│                                 │  │ Name: _____ │
│ Owner's Name: _____  │  │ Education: _____ │
│                                 │  │ Past Experience: Long Ago: ____ │
│ Job Title: _____  │  │ Recently: _____ │
│                                 │  │ Currently: _____ │
│ Job Description: _____  │  └─────────────────────────────────┘
│ _____  │  ┌─────────────────────────────────┐
│                                 │  │          Applicant #2           │
│ Job Requirement: _____  │  │ Name: _____ │
│ _____  │  │ Education: _____ │
│                                 │  │ Past Experience: Long Ago: ____ │
│ Job Requirement: _____  │  │ Recently: _____ │
│ _____  │  │ Currently: _____ │
│                                 │  └─────────────────────────────────┘
│ Job Requirement: _____  │  ┌─────────────────────────────────┐
│ _____  │  │          Applicant #3           │
│                                 │  │ Name: _____ │
│ Salary: _____  │  │ Education: _____ │
│                                 │  │ Past Experience: Long Ago: ____ │
│                                 │  │ Recently: _____ │
│                                 │  │ Currently: _____ │
└─────────────────────────────────┘  └─────────────────────────────────┘
```

## REPLICA OF *INTERVIEW! Resume Worksheet* FROM STUDENT WORKBOOK - PAGE 95

```
┌────────────────────────────────────────────────────────────────────────┐
│ Name: _____ Address: _____ Phone: _____         │
│ Education: High School; _____ College: _____        │
│            Graduate School: _____        │
│ First Job: _____       │
│ Last Job: _____       │
│ Current Job: _____       │
│ Special Skills & Talents: _____       │
└────────────────────────────────────────────────────────────────────────┘
```

# TARGET RANGE

## *NONE OF YOUR BUSINESS*
### Activity 7: Emergency!

**Practice Targets:** Discourse, Structures, Articulation, Time
**Level:** ★★★
**Group Size:** Large
**Repeat:** No
**Materials:** Student Workbook pages 96, 97, *None of Your Business* business cards, pencil (Optional: Costumes)
**Preparation:** Have business cards ready for distribution, arrange an area in the room for the Emergency stories.

**Background Information:** The Hampton Chapter of Commerce is sponsoring a workshop entitled *Handling Business Emergencies*. Each business has sent a representative to attend the workshop.

**Directions:** Distribute a business card to each student. Discuss and demonstrate the creation of a character, role play guidelines, and the invention of a name if necessary. Allow time for each student to create their characters.

After the business characters have been developed, each business representative will also develop a story about the worst emergency that has ever happened to their business.

**Story Requirements:**
1. Emergency stories should be three minutes in length.
2. The story should be told in sequence with a focus on describing what happened first, second, third, etc. Students will use the Student Workbook page as a guide for developing their stories. Instruct students to fill in the information in note form or use drawings which will enable them to remember the important points. English sentences should be avoided.
3. Each story should include the emergency, the actions they took, and what they would do differently if faced with a similar emergency.

136

# TARGET RANGE

## *NONE OF YOUR BUSINESS*
### Activity 7: Emergency!

When business representatives are ready, choose a student to go first. Encourage audience members to participate by asking clarifying questions at the end of the story.

**Note:**
To extend the activity as well as check for understanding, choose audience members to repeat the previously told emergency story and describe how they would handle that emergency.

### REPLICA OF *EMERGENCY!* FROM STUDENT WORKBOOK - PAGE 97

| Business Name: _____ | Owner's Name: _____ |
|---|---|
| **Sequence of Events** | |
| 1. | 5. |
| 2. | 6. |
| 3. | 7. |
| 4. | 8. |
| **Description of Actions** | |
| 1. | 3. |
| 2. | 4. |
| **What Would Be Done Differently** | |
| 1. | 3. |
| 2. | 4. |

# TARGET RANGE

## *NONE OF YOUR BUSINESS*
### Activity 8: Take 1!

**Practice Targets:** Structures, Articulation
**Level:** ★★★
**Group Size:** Small
**Repeat:** Yes
**Materials:** *None of Your Business* business card for each student, pencil (Optional Costumes)
**Preparation:** Have business cards ready for distribution

**Background Information:** The Hampton Better Business Bureau is sponsoring a television commercial contest in cooperation with the local cable access company. The winning business owner will receive a two week, all-expense paid trip for four to Hawaii. Each business is eagerly participating in the competition by creating their own one-minute television commercial.

**Directions:** Distribute a business card to each student. Discuss and demonstrate the creation of a character, role play guidelines, and the invention of a name if necessary. Allow time for each student to create their characters.

Inform students that each individual business representative will develop a one minute commercial for their business. The only stipulations to this assignment are that each business representative must be featured in their own commercial and the time be limited to one minute.

Allow students to create small *Commercial Support* groups. Explain that the purpose of these groups is to support the creative efforts of each of the members in the production of their commercials. Support can be offered in the form of brainstorming, acting as director or acting in the commercial itself, revising the scripts or anything else that is helpful for the production of the commercials.

Allow ample time for the *Commercial Support* groups to plan each of the commercials. Assign performance dates and create a performance roster.

You may want to bring a video camera for the commercials or ask the business representatives to perform the commercials "live." Encourage creativity, costumes and fun! Bring popcorn on the designated date and enjoy the show!

**Note:**
To add to the fun, create a mock airline ticket, and bring a lei. Even a fresh pineapple can represent the award. After all of the commercials have been presented, call for a vote. Present the winner with the Hawaiian prize.

# TARGET RANGE

## *NONE OF YOUR BUSINESS*
**Activity 9: Merger!**

**Practice Targets:** Discourse, Structures, Articulation
**Level:** ★★★
**Group Size:** Small
**Repeat:** No
**Materials:** Student Workbook pages 99, 100, *None of Your Business* business cards, nametags, pencil
**Preparation:** Have business cards ready for distribution, arrange room so that students can mingle to discuss mergers.

**Background Information:** Area business representatives are attending a trade show. Each of the business representatives is looking to increase the marketability and profits of their business. Representatives attending the trade show are seriously considering merging with one or more companies.

**Directions:** DAY 1: THE PLAN

Distribute a business card and a nametag to each student. Instruct students to write their character's name and business on the nametag. Discuss and demonstrate the creation of a character, role play guidelines, and the invention of a name if necessary. Allow time for each student to create their characters.

Arrange the room so that students can mingle. List the companies present on the board. Instruct students to look at the Student Workbook page and use it as a guide as they imagine the kinds of mergers they could create.

Students can mingle when ready. As they introduce themselves, encourage students to explore creative and unique mergers, as well as the products they could manufacture or the services their new company could provide.

When business representatives are ready to discuss a merger, instruct them to move to another part of the room and begin developing their ideas. Up to four businesses can merge. Mergers must be plausible and beneficial to each of the businesses involved. Students can use the form on the Student Workbook page to direct the process of the merger.

# TARGET RANGE

## *NONE OF YOUR BUSINESS*
### Activity 9: Merger!

**Day 2     THE PRESENTATIONS**

When each merger is complete, instruct groups to prepare a presentation for the class. Presentations should include all of the items from the Student Workbook. Each business owner should participate in the presentation and explain how this merger benefits their company.

Encourage students to use props and costumes to make the presentations more lively.

### REPLICA OF *MERGER* FROM STUDENT WORKBOOK - PAGE 100

```
Name of your business:_____        Partner's business _____
Partner's business _____            Partner's business _____
         Name of New Business:                         Target Audience:
         _____                       _____

Project Description: _____
            _____

Marketing Plan: _____
            _____
            _____

Cost to manufacture:   Wholesale Cost:   Retail Cost:   Profitability:   Sales Projections:
_____        _____     _____    _____     _____

                            Board of Directors
         President:         Vice President:                Secretary/Treasurer
         _____        _____              _____
```

# INDEX

**Readiness**
- An Evening of Amateur Mime 118
- And Who Are You? 31
- Charades with Feeling 19
- Develop a Survey 35
- It's a Gift for You 16
- Now You See It, Now You Don't 37
- Signal Flags 11
- Signs of the Times 14
- Story Groups 23
- The House that Jack Built 18
- What's Inside? 39
- Which Way? 9

**Discourse**
- And Who Are You? 31
- Categories 40
- Chamber of Commerce Meeting 120
- Charades with Feeling 19
- Chore Chart 57
- Cocktail Party 109
- Dayrunning 47
- Develop a Survey 35
- Emergency! 136
- Employment Agency Networking 60
- Errands 122
- Family Business 90
- Gretchen's "To Do" List 58
- Healing Stones 64
- Help Wanted! 132
- How Much, How Many Survey 76
- Hypochondriac 69
- Interview! 134
- It's a Gift for You 16
- Jen & Maggie's Schedule 44
- Kiddie Kare "Faux Pas" 54
- McGreevey Family Reunion 94
- McGreevey Family Tree 91
- Meet the McGreevy Family 88
- Merger! 139
- Miracle Cures! 69
- Mother's Nature Remedies 66
- Networking 101
- Oils & Aromas 62
- Outpatient Clinic 45
- Out to Lunch 78
- Panel Discussion 105
- Personal Family Trees 89
- Personal Time Lines 79
- Project 580 / Deaf Studies 111
- Roommate Wanted 129
- Signal Flags 11
- Signs of the Times 14
- Story Groups 23
- Student Interview 108
- The House that Jack Built 18
- The Weekend 80
- Twenty Year Reunion 55
- Wacko Weddings 81
- What's Inside? 39
- Which Way? 9
- Who Owns the Gallery? 42

**Time**
- Chore Chart 57
- Dayrunning 47
- Emergency! 136
- Employment Agency Networking 60
- How Much, How Many Survey 76
- Hypochondriac 69
- Interview! 134
- Jen & Maggie's Schedule 44
- Kiddie Kare "Faux Pas" 54
- Miracle Cures! 69
- Mother's Nature Remedies 66
- Outpatient Clinis 45
- Out to Lunch 78
- Personal Time Lines 79
- Twenty Year Reunion 55

**Numerals**
- Chore Chart 57
- Dayrunning 47
- Help Wanted! 132
- How Much, How Many Survey 76
- Hypochondriac 69
- Jen & Maggie's Schedule 44
- Kiddie Kare "Faux Pa"s 54
- Meet the McGreevy Family 88
- Miracle Cures! 69
- Mother's Nature Remedies 66
- Networking 101
- Outpatient Clinics 45
- Out to Lunch 78
- The Weekend 80
- Twenty Year Reunion 55

**Articulation**
- And Who Are You? 31
- Categories 40
- Chamber of Commerce Meeting 120
- Chore Chart 57

Cocktail Party   109
Dayrunning   47
Develop a Survey   35
Emergency!   136
Employment Agency Networking   60
Errands   122
Family Business   90
Gretchen's "To Do" List   58
Healing Stones   64
Help Wanted!   132
How Much, How Many Survey   76
Hypochondriac   69
Interview!   134
Jen & Maggie's Schedule   44
Kiddie Kare "Faux Pas"   54
McGreevey Family Reunion   94
McGreevey Family Tree   91
Merger!   139
Miracle Cures   69
Mother's Nature Remedies   66
Networking   101
Now You See It, Now You Don't   37
Oils & Aromas   62
Outpatient Clinic   45
Out to Lunch   78
Panel Discussion   105
Personal Family Trees   89
Personal Time Lines   79
Project 580 / Deaf Studies   111
Roommate Wanted   129
Signal Flags   11
Student Interview   108
Take 1!   138
The Weekend   80
Twenty Year Reunion   55
Wacko Weddings   81
What's Inside?   39
Which Way?   9
Who Owns the Gallery?   42

## Descriptors

Hypochondriac   69
It's a Gift for You   16
McGreevey Family Reunion   94
Meet the McGreevey Family   88
Miracle Cures!   69
Now You See It, Now You Don't   37
Personal Family Trees   89
Signal Flags   11
Signs of the Times   14
Story Groups   23
The House that Jack Built   18
Wacko Weddings   81
Which Way?   9
Who Owns the Gallery?   42

## Structures

And Who Are You?   31
Categories   40
Chamber of Commerce Meeting   120
Chore Chart   57
Cocktail Party   109
Dayrunning   47
Develop a Survey   35
Emergency!   136
Employment Agency Networking   60
Errands   122
Family Business   90
Gretchen's "To Do" List   58
Healing Stones   64
Help Wanted!   132
How Much, How Many Survey   76
Hypochondriac   69
Interview!   134
Kiddie Kare "Faux Pas"   54
McGreevey Family Reunion   94
McGreevey Family Tree   91
Meet the McGreevy Family   88
Merger!   139
Miracle Cure!s   69
Mother's Nature Remedies   66
Networking   101
Now You See It, Now You Don't   37
Oils & Aromas   62
Outpatient Clinics   45
Out to Lunch   78
Panel Discussion   105
Personal Family Trees   89
Personal Time Lines   79
Project 580 / Deaf Studies   111
Roommate Wanted   129
Student Interview   108
Take 1!   138
The Weekend   80
Twenty Year Reunion   55
Wacko Weddings   81
Who Owns the Gallery?   42